D0461885

50 WAYS TO MAKE GOOGLE LOVE YOUR WEBSITE

50 WAYS TO MAKE GOOGLE LOVE YOUR WEBSITE

Steve Johnston and Liam McGee

BUSINESS
BOOKS

Published by Random House Business Books 2010

2 4 6 8 10 9 7 5 3 1

Copyright © Steve Johnston and Liam McGee 2010

Steve Johnston and Liam McGee have asserted their rights under the Copyright, Designs and Patents Act, 1988, to be identified as the authors of this work

First published in Great Britain in 2010 by
Random House Business Books
Random House, 20 Vauxhall Bridge Road,
London SW1V 2SA

www.rbooks.co.uk

Addresses for companies within The Random House Group Limited can be found at: www.randomhouse.co.uk/offices.htm

The Random House Group Limited Reg. No. 954009

A CIP catalogue record for this book
is available from the British Library

ISBN 9781905211258

The Random House Group Limited supports The Forest Stewardship Council (FSC), the leading international forest certification organisation. All our titles that are printed on Greenpeace approved FSC certified paper carry the FSC logo. Our paper procurement policy can be found at
www.rbooks.co.uk/environment

Typeset by SX Composing DTP, Rayleigh, Essex

Printed and bound in Great Britain by
CPI Bookmarque, Croydon

TABLE OF CONTENTS

5 Build Your Website for Google 126

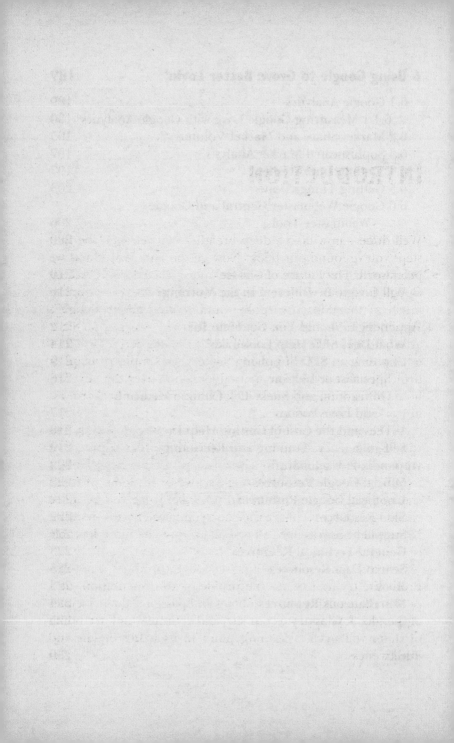

INTRODUCTION

Well done – now take a deep breath – you've taken the first step: you've found our book. Now get on and read it and we promise that very soon you will feel more relaxed about making Google love your website. This is possible because – contrary to much of the nonsense spoken and written about Google's search engine – there are no mysteries to investigate, no black arts to dispel and no secrets to uncover. Google decides whether or not to love a site by using some very simple principles: principles that you will come to understand over the next few hours of reading, regardless of your experience or background in working with websites.

As you begin to get to grips with the way Google works, you will learn how to use these principles in the development of your own website, and you will start appreciating how changes to your site will improve Google's love of it. Some of these changes will be straightforward to make; some will be more challenging because of the time and commitment they require. None will be impossible. All will make your site more loveable to Google.

Be it a commercial site selling services or products, a not-for-profit site trying to raise the profile of an organisation, or a personal site talking about hobbies and passions, the principles of Google's love apply to your site, and your new understanding of them will mark a turning point in its management and effectiveness.

WHY IS THIS BOOK NEEDED?

Google's love is an analogy for its preference for a website within its search results. The more Google loves a site, the more often it is presented as a potentially useful site to searchers, and the more visits that site can expect as a result. And because of Google's remarkable reach – it serves more than 1 billion searches every day[1] or 10.7% of all web visits[2] – it can regularly become the single biggest source of visitors to a website, a matter of great significance if you are trying to reach an audience or potential customers online.

Google's role in the creation of customer traffic to websites around the world makes understanding how it decides on its preferences a critical organisational issue. Google's power to make or break web businesses by the presence or lack of love for them is sufficient to justify the existence of a book such as this: a book which seeks to help you understand the nature of Google's preferences so that you can help it love your site better. There is, however, an additional reason why this book is needed: in the frontier town of 'Making Google Love Your Website', there are many snake oil salesmen, against whom a rational understanding of Google is your best defence.

The accepted, generic description of the services offered to help Google (and other search engines, such as Yahoo, Microsoft's Bing and Ask) love your website is Search Engine Optimisation, or SEO. SEO is an acronym that you may already be familiar with, and it is one that will make frequent appearances in this book.

If you find that, despite our efforts, this book has not answered your question, we'd encourage you to just 'google' it.

---

[1] There is no reliable source for this data, as Google refuses to share.
[2] Source: Experian Hitwise, Market share of UK visits to Google properties during November 2009

WHO ARE THE AUTHORS?
Steve Johnston

Steve is an ageing inhabitant of the online frontier towns of 'Why Do I Need a Website', 'E-commerce Is Small Now, But Just You Wait' and 'Dot-com Boom Time'. Presently he is living in 'Making Google Love Your Website', running a small consulting practice[1] as a Google consultant (you can follow him on http://twitter.com/stevejohnston). He likes to think that he's acquired a bit of wisdom in the course of the career he embarked on in 1994, which was very much a leap of faith in what the newly-invented World Wide Web (the web) was going to do for business. Most of his contribution to websites during these years has been as an independent voice encouraging common sense, vision and strategy to organisations struggling with their adoption of the web. He'll bend your ear, given half a chance, and point out that his first website offering such services was online to be archived for posterity when the Internet Archive began its Wayback Machine[2] in 1996.

It wasn't that he thought he was necessarily qualified to make such a contribution – he simply couldn't help himself. He had a hands-on interest in computer technology that had begun in high school at the end of the 1970s, and he found a use for it in everything he subsequently did in business during the late 1980s and early 1990s, from networking to CD-ROMS by way of EPoS[3]. When the web arrived, it seemed an obvious extension of computing's contribution to business: already managing data and transaction processing in the background, it could now process the communication channel between consumers and business. The day he first wrestled an internet connection into life in the summer of 1994 – and it really needed wrestling in those days –

---

[1] Search Johnston, Google Consultants: http://www.searchjohnston.co.uk
[2] http://web.archive.org/web/19961222182749/http://www.johnston.co.uk/
[3] Electronic Point of Sale – retail computer systems used to track sales and stocks.

and browsed the web page of a university lecturer in California (complete with a lovely photographic portrait of his young son) from his London suburb, is etched in his memory as a moment of real wonder. He has remained passionate about the web ever since.

Steve is also old enough to have had a pre-web career, and the call of a frontier town was irresistible then too. Having spent a couple of years as a bookselling apprentice after his time at university (studying psychology), in the following seven years he attempted to create a high street bookselling group from scratch in South London. Ultimately he wasn't successful, making a number of first-business mistakes that were largely obscured by the excesses of the boom of the late 1980s, but which were cruelly exposed by the subsequent recession.

Where Steve lacks conspicuous business success, he takes comfort in the value of experience. And yes, that was him on *Dragons' Den*[1] in 2006 taking a brief holiday in the frontier town of 'Web 2.0 User-Generated Recommendations', but that is a story for another time.

Steve is married with three teenage children and lives near the Roman city of Bath, in the south-west of the UK.

Liam McGee

Liam is the younger and (he would argue) handsomer part of this authorial duo. A Cambridge-educated scientist, his academic interests range across information retrieval, experimental psychology, communication theory, text mining and mathematical relationship modelling, all of which have come in mighty handy when working at the cutting edge of search engine optimisation. His academic interest in dinosaurs has so far come in less handy, but he lives in hope.

Liam's expertise in Google grew directly from his specialism in web accessibility. Web accessibility is the art of making the

---

[1] http://www.youtube.com/watch?v=HDczbpIO85g

web easy to read, understand and use for everyone – mobile phone users, older users, people with disabilities[1]. And last, and certainly not least: Google.

A chance meeting with Steve over a beer and a website project in 2004 made it clear that Liam's obsession with the clarity, meaning and structural perfection of websites made him a natural fit for Steve's growing Google consultancy business. Liam has been working closely with Steve ever since.

Liam has plenty of real-world understanding as well as theoretical grounding. He has well over a decade of practical commercial experience in specifying, designing, templating, producing, usability testing and maintaining websites for clients large and small. This continues to the present day through his work with Paul Ratcliffe at their web accessibility firm, Communis Ltd (you can follow him on http://twitter.com/liammcgee).

He is passionate about making the web better, and gives his Friday afternoons up to being a working group 'invited expert' for the W3C's Web Accessibility Initiative[2], and has done so for several years.

Liam is married and lives in Somerset, UK, with wife, one dog, four chickens and 50,000 bees.

ACKNOWLEDGEMENTS

We would like to take this opportunity of thanking our wives Sarah and Pia for their remarkable support during the challenge of writing this book. Our thanks also go to our colleagues Roland Dunn, Philip Read and Paul Ratcliffe for their patience while we have disappeared from the work radar to focus on writing and for their enormous contribution to our

---

[1] Who use a variety of exciting technology to get on the web, including software that reads out loud to blind users, voice-based input, screen magnifiers, colour filters, crazy mice and keyboards, and plenty more besides.

[2] If you've never visited, fire up a browser and go now to http.//www.w3.org/WAI/ .

collective understanding of Google's love, much of which has made it on to these pages. We'd like to thank Andrew Rosenheim for his belief in the e-book that was the progenitor of this edition and for his introduction to Nigel Wilcockson at Random House, whose patience has proved to be more than a match for Steve's ability to miss a deadline. Further acknowledgements go to Paul Mutton for a computing second opinion and to Anthony House from Google's communications team, who we offer a big thank you to for his help with fact-checking and permissions. Finally, Ken McGaffin deserves a special mention, without whom this book would be called something rather less engaging.

1
GETTING TO KNOW GOOGLE

It may already be obvious to you why Google is important and why making it love your website should be such a key objective, in which case please feel free to jump forward to chapter 2 How Does Google Work? If, on the other hand, you'd like a little scene-setting and some background to this book, please read on.

1.1 GOOGLE'S FOUNDING AND PHILOSOPHY

Google was born of a doctorate research project at the computer science department of Stanford University in California, USA, in 1997. The project, conceived by Larry Page and Sergey Brin, was established to research new ways to provide quality search results from the masses of information found on the web. Their passion for solving this problem overtook their studies and they left the university to establish a company to create the world's best search engine. At this time they had little idea about how the business would make money, but they had faith that their determination to produce the best and fastest results would be rewarded.

Page and Brin were convinced that they were taking an approach to search that was fundamentally different and considerably more sophisticated than any of the other search engines available at the time, most notably Yahoo and Altavista. This conviction was based on the following elements of their approach:

- They were applying many more factors to the 'understanding' of the information their software found on websites and its likely usefulness to searchers.
- They had conceived of a unique citation model that assessed the relative usefulness of a web page by the links that pointed to it from elsewhere on the web. These citations were considered to be votes of confidence, and the inclusion of this model was their major breakthrough.

The name Google was applied to the project while it was in its research phase at Stanford and comes from a misspelling of the word googol. A googol is a very large number (the digit 1 followed by a hundred zeros), and the word was used by Page and Brin to hint at the very large amounts of data their search engine would process. However, after realising their mistake, they discovered that the domain name googol.com had already been registered, so they decided to stick with Google anyway.

Google was originally conceived as a technology business that would license its search engine software to other companies to generate revenue; however, early attempts at this were not very successful. Nonetheless, Google was quickly acquiring everyday users who were enjoying the quality and speed of the results at Google.com, and who, by the end of 1999, were executing 7 million searches per day[1].

Google's lack of income was compounded by the dot-com bubble bursting early in 2000, when many of Google's potential customers suddenly ceased to exist or had significantly reduced funds available for such a licence. Despite Page and Brin's focus on the search software itself, they had to find a revenue stream quickly or they could suffer the same fate as many of their dot-com peers. Advertising was seen as the answer to their problems; however, they were very nervous about the impact it

---

[1] David A. Vise, *The Google Story*, Delta, 2008, page 85

would have on their users and on the perceived independence of their results. By this time Page and Brin had adopted the corporate philosophy of 'Don't be Evil'; reconciling advertising with their purist approach to the best possible search results under such a mantle seemed inconceivable to them.

An encounter with the precursor business to Yahoo Search Marketing (GoTo.com, which became Overture Inc. before Yahoo acquired it) convinced Page and Brin otherwise. GoTo.com was a search engine where advertisers paid to have their adverts shown when users typed in relevant search expressions. It seemed possible to Page and Brin that they could provide something similar, with highly focused adverts based on the search terms users typed in. They decided to place the adverts alongside the main search results of Google.com, clearly marked as 'sponsored' results. The value that this model would provide was then enhanced by an auction model to determine whose paid advert would appear at the top of the sponsored results.

By the end of 2000 Google had settled on a business model that has remained virtually unchanged – the best search results accompanied by relevant adverts – and which by the end of 2001 had earned its first annual trading profit of US$7 million (which by the end of 2009 had grown to US$6.5 billion).

Google had also started talking about a mission to organise the world's information and make it universally accessible and useful. Note here that Google is not just talking about the information on the web: it really is after the world's information, and couples that with a mission to ensure it is doing a useful job, which means producing quality results that are genuinely relevant to a user's needs. Google has held true to this mission and continues to innovate and deliver free services to users that help achieve these goals, with the financial success of the business providing considerable resources to pursue the mission further.

1.2 ORGANISING THE WORLD'S INFORMATION

Google's ambition to give the people of the world free access to all the information in the world is stunning in its scale. Yet, this does appear to be what Google is trying to do, albeit at an understandably slow pace in some areas, such as the scanning of books. Google has gone about developing and acquiring more and more services that organise more and more of the world's information, working on the assumption that alongside all the information they organise there will be a willing associate in the form of an advertiser who is prepared to pay to be there. The list of Google's current services that involve organisation and search includes the following:

- Web search
- Image search
- Blog search
- News search
- Video search (Google Video and YouTube)
- Map search (and Google Earth)
- Shopping search (of retail or submitted databases)
- Book search (actually from scanning the print editions of books)
- Goggles search (using image recognition as the query)
- Mail (which includes search and adverts)
- Docs (which includes word processor, calendar, spreadsheets, etc.)
- Picasa (photo image organisation with Picasa Web Albums sharing and storage)
- Analytics (service that helps analyse traffic to websites)
- Talk (instant messaging and voice software)
- Orkut (social network)
- Groups (forums)
- Directory (categorised listings of websites, based on the Open Directory Project[1])

---

[1] http://www.dmoz.org

- Base (a service that allows users to publish information of any kind directly on Google services)
- Desktop (a version of Google's search software that searches your computer)
- Translate (language services that translate submitted content or web pages)
- Chrome (a web browser, like Firefox or Internet Explorer)
- Blogger (a blog publishing and hosting service)
- Android (a mobile-phone operating system)
- Checkout (a service offering secure online payment)
- Search Appliance (search engine software for your site – i.e. the original business model)

Despite this growing range of services, the majority of Google's activity and, therefore, revenue comes from web search, which is the area of focus for this book. It is where users mostly experience Google's effectiveness at organising the world's information, when their needs are satisfied by a few words typed into Google. It is also where most of its wide-ranging work goes on to assess the usefulness of the information it has found on the web.

Google is not yet a victim of its own success, but its ubiquity causes it to be a target for every unethical business on the planet that may seek to acquire customers through it. Google's scale of use makes any small slice of the searches made by its users – all 8 billion of them in October 2008 in the US alone[1] – worth pursuing with some aggression for those who don't mind bending the rules. The consequence is that Google has to invest more and more in technology and processes to reduce the risk of showing the sites of such unscrupulous operators. These processes are constantly being refined but remain based on Google's core methodology for assessing the information it finds

---

[1] Source: Comscore http://www.comscore.com/

on the web and its potential usefulness to users. Google is constantly on the lookout for sites that attempt to cheat their way into its results, while allowing legitimate sites with a good reputation to feature.

Google's organising methodology therefore has two main functions:

1. Indexing: identifying the types of information it finds, analysing it to establish what it is about, and creating a searchable database so that users can find the details within it.
2. Authenticating: assessing the relative usefulness of the information it has in its index by evaluating the references each piece enjoys, as measured by the quality of the links to it.

This process of indexing and authenticating is at the heart of Google's web search and is applied widely to many of its other services. How well Google achieves this process is at the heart of its success; the better it understands the usefulness of the information it finds, the better its results will be and the happier its users will be. The next chapter will cover Google's processes in more detail; for now, it is enough to appreciate that Google's pursuit of quality results is second to no other consideration in the business. The minute Google compromises the relevance of its results to its users' needs is the minute they open the door to a competitor.

The relevance of Google's results to its users' needs is what keeps them coming back every day, and that, combined with the effectiveness of its system of presenting relevant advertisements, means relevance keeps Google in business. Understanding how hard it is for Google to maintain its assessments of the relevance and usefulness of web content is an important step towards understanding what it takes to create websites that are as consistent with its efforts as they possibly can be. And nothing demonstrates the scale of its efforts more than the challenge of the 'long tail' of search. Google is not very forthcoming about exactly how many web pages it has in its search database, but industry anecdote suggests it must be in the region of 100 billion unique pages. Frankly, the figure is not particularly useful because it is impossible to comprehend that much information. It is, however, Google's task to match these pages to the hundreds of millions of search expressions that users type into Google every day.

Most people expect these searches to be composed of largely predictable needs: 'flights to paris', 'cheap lcd tvs', 'cinemas in bristol', 'doctor who episodes', 'hangover cures', etc. What they are not prepared for is the fact that, on a daily basis, 20% of them have NEVER been typed into Google before. Never. That's right: if only 100 different things were typed into Google every day, 20 of them would be brand new to Google. And, apparently, Google will never see most of those 20 ever again[1].

This incomprehensibly huge stream of demands on Google amounts to a remarkable window into people's souls – something likened to a database of intentions by search commentator John Battelle[2] – and is such a long and ever-changing list of needs that only a piece of huge and sophisticated technical wizardry could hope to do anything useful with it. The patterns of relative volumes across this window, when ordered on a scale by volume, produces what is referred to as a 'long tail' curve (see illustration 1 overleaf). Here, despite the huge volumes of searches for the really popular stuff in the head of the tail like 'ipods', 'twitter' and 'obama' there is actually more overall volume in the tail. Even though the searches occurring in the tail have relatively low volumes

---

[1] Google have 'in fact' said two separate things: 20–25% of unique expressions are brand new daily, and 20% of all queries haven't been seen for 90 days. We've used some editorial licence to arrive at the figure in the text above.

[2] John Battelle, *The Search*, Nicholas Brearley Publishing, Chapter 1

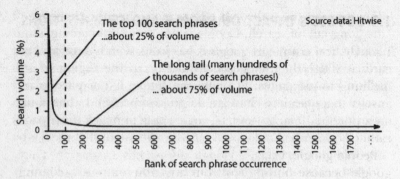

Illustration 1: A long tail

per search in any period of time, the sheer length of the tail – the almost endless variety of the things people ask of Google – ultimately produces more searches in total than the popular terms in the head, and the further one travels along it, the more refined and specific – and low in volume – the searches become. What does a long tail search look like, you may ask? How about: 'best small business anti virus solutions', 'boys ballet best age to start', '48cm wide fridge freezers in silver', 'apartments with view of river and golf in US' and 'agricultural conferences in scotland uk in april 2009'. While these specific examples may not look familiar to you, their form surely does. Everyone does long tail searches at some point, because they often want something quite specific, and the more they refine their search, the more success they experience (on the whole). It probably won't surprise you also to learn that the more specific users get – that is, the more they qualify their needs – the more likely they are to become a customer of the sites Google refers them to.

Google's organisation of the world's information is a computing task on a scale never seen before: hundreds of billions of pages of information matched, in real time, with hundreds of millions of unique searches, in a profoundly useful way.

1.3 GOOGLE'S IMPACT ON PEOPLE AND ORGANISATIONS

I google, you google, he googles, she googles, etc. Chronicled as early as 2001[1], the use of 'google' as a verb is now ubiquitous[2], meaning to engage with Google in the simplest way to get an answer to a question, or locate a suitable product, or check up on a potential employee/date, or a whole bunch of stuff we'd rather not mention.

People google, because Google always has an answer. They google because finding stuff out any other way is becoming much slower and harder almost all the time. Few people bother to remember web addresses of companies any more, as is evident from the googling of company names, when those company web addresses are almost exactly the same as their names. In fact, often it is not that people can't remember the web addresses of the sites they want to visit, they type a company name into Google because this gets them there faster and more reliably than typing a company web address into the address bar of their web browser.

There was a time when people who typed things like 'Dell' or 'BBC' into Google were regarded as inexperienced users who didn't really understand the difference between a Google search box and the address bar, but as time has moved on such practice has become accepted as a further sign of Google's effectiveness and something everyone indulges in regularly. This behaviour is referred to as navigational search; in other words, it is a website navigation choice by users.

It is already hard to remember what it was like in the late 1990s, when web search was desperately ineffective and the amounts of information available online were relatively small.

---

[1] 'Don't Be Shy, Ladies – Google Him!', *New York Observer*, http://www.observer.com/node/43860

[2] Something Google is wrestling with (see http://googleblog.blogspot.com/2006/10/do-you-google.html).

Now, because Google has become so effective, googling is most people's way of choice into the current mass of stuff on the web, and it is proving a remarkably efficient means of finding information. Using Google is becoming a form of dependency – a dependency that no doubt delights Google, but one that causes all sorts of difficulties for other organisations. A corollary of this dependence is Google's growing control and influence over much of the way people find and choose the answers to their needs, be they for health information, public services, travel plans, shopping or entertainment.

While history shows how influential broadcast advertising was in the pre-digital, pre-multichannel world, it was, however, only an 'influence'; people were completely free from the point of influence onwards to choose the next step on their customer journey. Google's difference is that not only do its judgements about which sites are most likely to be useful influence people's decision-making, it then goes on to mediate the relationship between users and the sites themselves by delivering them directly to the point of most likely use. Of course they are still free to choose the next steps in their journeys, but Google makes its suggested next step irresistibly simple and compelling. Such mediation of demand and supply on Google's scale is a form of market control that is without precedent, and a form of control that continues to take many businesses by surprise. Such a surprise may in fact be the reason you are reading this book. The impact of this mediation on organisations, particularly ones who are run by people whose experience is mostly from the pre-web world, is a forced change to the way they think about customer acquisition. Regardless of whether you are a commercial or non-commercial organisation, the people who are crossing your virtual threshold are turning more and more to Google to help them decide where to go and what to do. An understanding of Google's role in the way your customers hunt out the answers to their needs is therefore no longer optional; it has become an organisational essential, the absence of which may bring into question your fitness for purpose and your future prospects.

Google has become so important in some business sectors, particularly those where the majority of purchases are now happening online – the travel sector, for example – that it can control the destiny of a third of a total market, assuming that Google is responsible for approximately 50% of the visitors to sites in that market, which it often is. Such conditions call for extraordinary efforts by organisations to ensure their websites and their content are considered both relevant and authentic by Google at every level. When you consider that Google has been a force on the web since 2001 you may find yourself wondering why organisations are still struggling to do this. The answer is that they are struggling because it is really hard. Understanding how Google works – as you will discover in the next chapter – requires an unusual combination of technical, editorial, marketing, communication and relationship skills, which rarely exist together in one place. Getting to grips with Google in the organisation has echoes of getting to grips with the web in the mid-1990s; an unusual combination of expertise was required then too, which simply didn't exist within organisations – in fact, technology and marketing were frequently in different buildings or countries, making it well-nigh impossible to combine their expertise.

Google's penetration into the organisation has found one channel through marketing and advertising executives, who have embraced Google's sponsored search results – called AdWords[1] – because, one assumes, it is a model they are familiar with: paying to get noticed. It has some subtleties and complexities in Google's version, but advertising is the responsibility of a single department managing a single budget, and advertising on Google is something that is close to being understood by organisations all over the planet. This understanding, however,

---

[1] http://adwords.google.com/

does not help to make the organisation's website feature as a real search result – that is, a non-sponsored, non-paid, natural result, where Google is considering it both relevant and authentic – because there is very little overlap between AdWords and Google's natural search results.

Alongside a growth in awareness of Google's role in mediating supply and demand online, we are witnessing a growth in determination, within the organisations we meet in the course of our consulting work, to make more strenuous efforts to win Google's love, particularly where they can no longer ignore the scale of its influence. They are enjoying varying levels of success with the resources available to them, and their efforts have the right motivation at their heart: to learn how to approach the problem and to apply their learning in the most cost-effective manner possible. It is hard not to be disappointed, however, with the quality of the teaching they have received to date – demonstrating a problem with supply in the market for practitioners knowledgeable about Google – which is a big part of our motivation to write this book: to document a simple and methodical approach to understanding Google and a practical approach to applying that understanding to websites so that Google learns to love them more.

It is now the case that most visits to most areas of interest on the web come from Google-referred traffic. This sees Google responsible for nearly 40% of all visits to all sites[1] and despite being the website people use to find where to go, rather than a website they stay on, it also is the busiest website in most of the markets it serves[2].

---

[1] Source: Experian Hitwise, Upstream traffic to All Categories of websites, November 2009

[2] Source: Experian Hitwise, Internet visit data for the UK, USA, Australia, Canada and Brazil, November 2009

2

HOW DOES GOOGLE WORK?

Google has a huge and sophisticated piece of technical wizardry running its web search and if you are hoping for a mathematical deconstruction of the algorithm at the heart of it, you are going to be disappointed by this chapter. Our intended audience for this book is not one that is likely to be able to make a whole lot of sense of the beautiful equation at the heart of Google's PageRank[1]:

$$\pi^T = \pi^T (\alpha S + (1-\alpha)E)$$

Because, let's face it, there are few who can. We are reliably informed[2] that its beauty almost qualifies it for a place in the museum of great equations, should such a thing exist. If mathematics is not your strong point, you needn't worry, because getting Google to love your website does not require an understanding of mathematical equations, let alone the professorial ability that is required to truly appreciate what is going on in that one. This chapter will instead attempt to translate the sophistication at the heart of Google's search

---

[1] Those of you more familiar with the mathematics of PageRank will have noticed that this isn't the simple summation equation commonly associated with PageRank. This equation is the final form of the PageRank equation that accommodates the reducible and teleportation matrices S and E and the PageRank vector of the Google matrix π.

[2] Amy Langville and Carl Meyer, *Google's PageRank and Beyond*, Princeton University Press, 2006

engine into simple concepts that will help you understand the principles at work and how they must affect the way you build your website if you want more of its love.

2.1 THE WISDOM OF CROWDS

The main breakthrough Google achieved in its approach to creating a search engine was to make use of a principle born out of academic publishing. A 'citation' is a reference to a source – such as a research paper – from within an article on the same topic. The quantity of citations a source acquires following its publication is considered a measure of its quality, relevance and usefulness. The founders of Google decided that such a measure could be applied to the information it found on the web, where the citations were not simple textual references to other sources, but the actual web links that exist from one web page to another. The assumption was that the more links that existed to a particular web page, the more this could be interpreted as an indication of that page's quality, relevance and usefulness. If handled at an automated level, an assessment of each page's individual usefulness could be achieved.

Usefulness is at the heart of Google's mission (to organise the world's information and make it universally accessible and useful), and without useful results we would quickly abandon Google's web search for an alternative. Usefulness, in Google's eyes, is a combination of the relevance and authority that a website or web page has with regard to a particular search that a user may make. It is, however, extremely hard to assess these things automatically using computer technology, because such assessments require judgements that are difficult for humans, even if they are experts, let alone for software that is yet to be imbued with human sensibilities.

Google's solution to the problem of assessing usefulness is beautifully simple and is based on a concept that has come to be known as the Wisdom of Crowds, thanks to a 2004 book by

James Surowiecki[1]. One of Surowiecki's examples explains the effectiveness of this approach. The English Victorian economist Sir Francis Galton, in an article[2] he wrote for the scientific journal *Nature* in 1907, expressed his surprise that the average values from 787 different entries in a competition to guess the likely butchered and dressed weight of a live ox presented at a country show was accurate to within 1% of the actual weight achieved after the animal had been slaughtered. His assessment of the value of this exercise was to assert that 'this result is more creditable to the trustworthiness of a democratic judgement than might have been expected'. Surowiecki's book goes on to argue that these collective democratic judgements are frequently more accurate than the judgements of a small number of supposed experts.

2.1.1 The Birth of Reputation

Galton assumed that 'the judgements [of the competitors] were unbiased by passion and uninfluenced by oratory and the like [with the] sixpenny fee deterring practical joking, and the hope of a prize and the joy of competition prompting each competitor to do his best'. Google originally assumed that the democratic judgements that brought links into being between websites were similarly unbiased, and before Google had any significant market share, this assumption was probably correct. Before Google, links only existed between sites for largely genuine reasons, where site owners wanted to refer visitors to other useful sources on the web. After Google, links acquired the power to influence the presentation of websites in its results, and, given Google's rapid growth, website owners

---

[1] James Surowiecki, *The Wisdom of Crowds: Why the Many Are Smarter Than the Few and How Collective Wisdom Shapes Business, Economies, Societies and Nations*, Little, Brown, 2004

[2] http://galton.org/essays/1900-1911/galton-1907-vox-populi.pdf?page=7

soon wised up to this. Google had to quickly combat the early – and often successful – attempts to bias its results by site owners who fabricated multiple new links from websites created solely for this purpose. It did so by learning not to trust the motives of website owners in their decisions to link to other sites (yes, that's right, Google doesn't trust you!) and by implementing a range of quality assessments of the sites on which it found links in order to decide if and how much it could trust them.

It decided that the best way to do this was to calculate a trust 'score' for each site and its links by considering two primary quality signals: their relevance to the target of the link and their authority within their pocket of relevance, known together as their 'Reputation'. Google has made these Reputation calculations very sophisticated, in order to make them hard to influence inappropriately and in order to take account of the huge scale of information involved, by ensuring they are highly sensitive to the particular search needs expressed by users. When considering how much value to attribute to a link, Google can give a site very high relevance scores for one topic, but very low ones for another, while its authority may also be high only on a particular topic (Google's calculation of these scores is explored in more detail in the following sections). This Reputation assessment can then be considered the 'true' value of the democratic judgement this site can pass on to the sites it chooses to link to, which in turn will be allowed to influence Google's assessment of the likely usefulness of those sites.

This is where it gets really clever: Google assesses the Reputation of a site by looking, in turn, at the relevance and authority of a site voting for it. In other words, sites acquire Reputation by the relevance and authority of the combined chain of sites linking to them, an assessment that continues recursively through the almost endless web of links (1 trillion known links between 100 billion pages) that exist, to arrive at a picture of the Reputation of all the sites on the web[1]. This assessment of the value of links from sites based on their relevance and authority is then factored into Google's decisions about how to rank the websites it shows to its users when they search for related information.

'School league tables' Reputation example

Let's look at a site with a wide-ranging and powerful reputation, such as that of the British Broadcasting Corporation (BBC) at www.bbc.co.uk, whose authority is born of the 600 million links it enjoys from the 1.25 million separate websites[2] that link to it. These sites, and their links, are not all equally trustworthy in Google's eyes, but they are likely to have some relevance to the content on the BBC site, either in general – to its role as the UK's public service broadcaster – or to the specific contents of a particular article on a unique web page. Using the BBC in an example of the Reputation (i.e., the relevance and authority) of websites and how they acquire it, will help explain these issues.

A small school website has a link from a news article on its site about its position in the government's school league tables to a page about these results in the education section of the BBC's website. In this example we will refer to the local school website as the source of the link and the BBC's site as the target of the link. When Google analyses the relevance of the page from the source site – the school's news article – to the page on the target site – the BBC's results article – it finds material that is

---

[1] If your mathematical brain is wondering how this actually works – where does Google start? – then we recommend Langville and Meyer's Princeton University Press publication referenced in the opening to this chapter.

[2] Majestic SEO data from January 2010

very consistent, such as the name and address of the school and the reference to league tables in the editorial. And when it evaluates the authority of the school site, it finds a small but significant pattern of separate source sites linking to it that are relevant either to the locality of the school – its town or village – or to its topic as a school – such as a link from a government educational site. Google doesn't, however, find any links to the school's website referring to its league table performance or to the specific article. Consequently, Google evaluates the school site to have high Reputation for its name and for the fact that it is actually a real school, but low Reputation for anything related to league tables. A link to the BBC's site from the school will therefore be very influential in Google's assessment of the usefulness of the target page for search expressions that contain the school's name but only marginally influential in its assessment of the usefulness of the target page for search expressions that contain references to league tables.

Google's breakthrough was the assessment of a site's Reputation – a 'true' reflection of the crowd of millions of democratic judgements that exist on the web (the world's collective wisdom) – in its calculations of the usefulness of websites, thereby enabling it to trust again.

2.2 RELEVANCE IS EVERYTHING TO GOOGLE

Google's use of the wisdom of the web crowd is critical to the millions of decisions it makes every day presenting searchers with useful, ranked results, yet it doesn't explain the 'Relevance' judgement it has to make in the first instance about every page it looks at on the web. In other words, what is that page actually about? And for what sorts of searches would it make sense to show it?

In computer science terms Google's search engine sits within a discipline called information retrieval, and as with the mathematical equation at the beginning of the chapter you may be glad to learn that we are not about to head off on a computer science tangent. We are, however, going to grapple with a few simple information retrieval principles that are behind the job Google is doing, because they are important for your understanding of Google and how to make it love your site; please don't skip this part.

At the heart of Google's search engine is some very sophisticated software that visits the web pages of the world and then decides what they are about. The principles it uses to make these decisions are relatively simple but their actual expression – as information retrieval processes – has to be refined, subtle and complex in order to deal with the magnitude of the information encountered on the web. The simple principles are enough for us to work with here, so what are they?

2.3 FINDING WEB PAGES

The first thing a web search engine has to do is to find the information it wants to include in its index – and remember Google really wants this information as part of its mission. Every piece of the web's information resides on what is called a web page and is identified by a unique address called a web address. This web address is more accurately called a URL, the acronym standing for Uniform Resource Locator, which simply means it is an unchanging (uniform) page (resource) finder (locator)[1] – such

---

[1] For the more technical reader: 'The term "Uniform Resource Locator" (URL) refers to the subset of Uniform Resource Identifiers that, in addition to identifying a resource, provide a means of locating the resource by describing its primary access mechanism (e.g., its network "location")'; source: http://labs.apache.org/webarch/uri/rfc/rfc3986.html#URLvsURN. We shall be using the URL convention throughout this book as it is URLs that Google indexes.

as http://www.bbc.co.uk/blogs/technology/2008/10/googles_good
_old_days.html. As long as this page of content is still available on
the BBC's site, this URL will continue to locate the information at
that address. Users, however, experience the web page itself and
may not even notice its specific URL – it is shown in the web
address bar of the web browser – yet the difference between a
user's perception of a web page and its specific URL is an
important distinction to make at this point. It is important because
Google has the opposite experience to users and sees only URLs,
not web pages, because that is how web pages actually exist: as
addressable locations on the internet at which content resides.

Google's hunt for information to put in its index therefore
becomes a hunt for URLs, and it finds them in most of the
pages on the web. On average, every page on the web links to
ten more web pages, which means that for every URL Google
visits it finds another ten to visit next. On most sites, the
majority of these URLs are to further locations on the same site
that Google already knows about, but some will lead it off to
visit other pages and sites that will be brand new to it, feeding
its voracious appetite for the world's information.

At this point, it is important to realise that when Google visits
a website, it is different from a user's visit to a website (that is, a
human being looking at the web using a browser, such as
Internet Explorer, Mozilla Firefox or Google Chrome). No,
Google doesn't use a browser like these, it has its own software
called Googlebot, and as the name suggests, this is a 'bot' or a
robot, not a human. Googlebot is an unmanned piece of software that automatically crawls the web's pages and links, that
doesn't need to sleep and doesn't need to work on its own.
Google has a dazzling number of bots working at any time,
which explains why it is possible for a single large site, such as
www.bbc.co.uk, to experience Googlebot visiting 100,000 URLs
every day. Yes, really. Given Google's ambition to organise the
world's information, it is easy to imagine how these bots are
going to be very busy, indefinitely.

Despite Google's power to mediate traffic on the web, its hunt for URLs is not always accommodated by websites. Even those sites who really want Google to love them seem oblivious to certain facts about the way Googlebot works. An example of how Googlebot is thwarted by many websites involves something called JavaScript. JavaScript is a widely used software programming language (strictly speaking, a scripting language) that supports the way web browsers work, particularly when doing more interactive things – like dragging Google's maps around with the mouse, or launching a YouTube video – and its capabilities are installed in web browsers by default. The problem for Googlebot is that it doesn't have the same JavaScript capabilities as a browser, so it does not execute all the processes on a website that requires them to be present. These issues may not seem too much of a problem where maps and videos are involved, but JavaScript finds its way into a lot of places where, for a happy Googlebot, it shouldn't. The simplest example of this is the use of website navigation buttons that do fancy things, like change colour or animate, when you click on them, before they take you to the next page on the site. The fancy stuff often requires JavaScript, and the web developer frequently forgets, when writing the JavaScript, that Googlebot cannot naturally get past it to find the URL for the next page. Thus the next page becomes invisible to Googlebot, and its contents will not appear in Google's search results, however relevant they may be.

JavaScript navigation buttons that don't show Google a URL are one example of how URLs and content become invisible to Google, which makes the discipline of making websites accessible to Googlebot one of Visibility. There are many other ways web pages make content inaccessible to Googlebot, which will be discussed in considerable detail in chapter 5 Build Your Website for Google.

So, for the pages Googlebot has found, its next job is to understand what they are about.

2.4 UNDERSTANDING WEB PAGES

When visiting a website, Google does not enjoy the advantages we humans do with their mental faculties at work. Human users, with their web browsers and their brains, experience the content presented to them in a form that they can make sense of.

For example, we see the web page as:

However, Google experiences this as:

Google experiences what is referred to as the 'source code' of a web page, which is the general name given to human-readable instructions that a computer can process. You can look at the source code of any web page you visit by selecting the 'View' option on your web browser toolbar and looking for an option that says something like 'Page Source'. In the case of the source code in web pages, the computer is being told to use the web browser to present the information in a specific way and enable functions, so that humans can understand and use the web page content in a form that is very familiar to them using just their eyes, their brain and their fingertips. However, Googlebot doesn't have eyes, let alone a brain or fingers. In fact Googlebot does nothing much with the source code it experiences at websites, other than retrieve what it can of it and deposit it in storage back at Google.

The source code of a web page is generally referred to as its HTML. While this may not always be the full story technically[1], its use as a generic label is helpful at this point to distinguish between what users see and what Google sees as a robot. HTML is another computer language – the HyperText Markup Language – that is used to describe the structure of the information on a web page, so that a web browser can present it effectively. So, to be clear: the source code of a web page is its HTML, and it is HTML that Google retrieves from websites.

Once the HTML from the URLs Googlebot has visited is placed in storage, a new process begins at Google that tries to make sense of it. The job of trying to understand what a page is about begins by identifying within the source code the stuff that relates to the information users see when they look at the page and the stuff that relates to the structure of the infor-mation and everything else that goes on in the page, such as layout elements that carry no information and code that makes buttons work. The information that users see is called the content of the page, and it is usually clearly described by the HTML (but not always, for reasons we shall explain).

---

[1] When using HTML in this section, we are largely referring, more specifically, to XHTML.

Having identified the content, Google then looks for information within the code that explains the structure and the relationship between the different pieces of content it finds (which is the most important, which bits relate to other bits, etc.). Once it has achieved this first process, it has a set of information that is both the content of the page and the relative importance it has within the page.

There are different ways that a piece of content on a page can be represented as important in the HTML; however, these different ways are not always consistent with the way they appear important to users when they look at them. For example, when humans look at a web page, the size of the text is a simple indication of its role and importance on the page, with the biggest text usually reserved for the most important headline. This makes sense to viewers of the page, but does not necessarily mean the same thing in the HTML. Many web designers focus their energies on making the content of a web page look right and work for human visitors, using whatever method they can to achieve design excellence, but while laudable in helping users of the site, it can be neglectful of Google's needs to understand it. Using this headline example, a web designer may be satisfied if the HTML says that the font size of the headline text should be 200% of the normal font size, but they may not bother to place the headline in a piece of HTML markup called a Heading 1 tag (which looks like <h1>{Headline}[1]</h1>). The difference to Google is profound: when only font size is used, Google may be able to determine that the information that is held at 200% of the normal font size is more important than the rest of the content on the page, but it is an ambiguous and unreliable signal; whereas, if the <h1> tag is used, Google is given a categoric indication of the role of this content – that it is the single most important set of words on the page and the primary topic of the content that follows, i.e. its semantic role. Web designers who

---

[1] Replacing {Headline} with the appropriate headline text in the site itself.

use heading tags to define the headlines in their web pages are not then denied the ability to make it 200% the size of the normal text; on the contrary, they are able to supplement the heading tag with presentation information, called a style marker, that tells the browser to show the content that is in a `<h1>` at 200% of the normal font size. With structure and style working together in this manner, both the web user and Google are satisfied.

Some of the information presented to visitors of a web page is capable of confounding Google further, or rather, as it transpires, Google can be blissfully ignorant of its existence. In the previous section, Finding Web Pages, we discussed Googlebot's ignorance of URLs it couldn't find because they are obscured by JavaScript navigation buttons, and this new example of a problem of 'Visibility' is just as simple: Google's ability to understand the contents of an image are very limited[1], so holding important information, such as words, in an image makes them invisible to Google. Important words on a web page are hidden in pictures more often than you might imagine, the most notable examples being those pesky navigation buttons again. In the pursuit of design control, a web designer may resort to presenting a website's navigation scheme as a set of images with words on them. These words, sadly, are suddenly rendered invisible to Google, which means they are not available to Google when it has to consider what the page is actually about. And considering how relevant the words on navigation buttons usually are to the content of a whole website, their lack of Visibility to Google can have a major effect on its perception of the site's Relevance to those words.

Approaching the Visibility and structure of the content of your web pages with Google in mind allows you to present it in a highly organised manner by utilising HTML to its fullest. The

---

[1] Late 2009, the only image content option Google Images offers is the identification of faces.

good news is that there is a set of very clear, agreed standards for how to provide Google with this Visibility and structure, and they are called Web Standards[1], which deliver the additional benefits of improved performance in other search engines and improved accessibility for users with disabilities. We shall explore how to comply with these standards in greater detail in chapter 5. Google is a great respecter of Web Standards, which means any site that desires Google's love must be one too.

2.5 BUILDING AN INDEX OF CONTENT

Once Google has retrieved the pages of information found at the URLs it has crawled, it builds an index of the visible content it found in the HTML. We hear a lot about Google's index of the web – but what is an index, exactly? Simply, it's a list of terms – just like the index of a book – which helps users locate information that is relevant to the individual terms. With a web index, when a search is made, Google doesn't look at every one of the URLs of content it has collected and check for the presence of the search terms. It checks instead against an index comprising a list of words. Attached to each word is a list of the URLs that contain the word. As there are far fewer words in any language than there are URLs on the web, this makes things a lot quicker. An index is therefore required so that Google can find the URLs again and refer searchers to them whenever it decides the content could be potentially useful.

An indexing process, at its simplest, is one where each URL is given a unique identification number which is then stored against each of the words found in the content of the page. On a URL by URL basis, the words will normally have been encountered before, so this process simply appends the unique number for this URL to the list of words that appear on it, along with all

---

[1] See http://en.wikipedia.org/wiki/Web_standards and http://www.webstandards.org/ for further information.

the other URLs that were found also to have these specific words. This then provides a simple look-up: a word is searched for and the index provides a list of URLs it appears on[1].

Because of the huge number of web pages Google considers in its 'usefulness' decisions, this indexing process needs to be incredibly sensitive to the differences that exist across pages so that the accuracy it achieves in matching searches with relevant pages is as high as it can be. A search engine that worked as simply as the list-of-words example above would become useless after a few hundred web pages, let alone a few hundred million.

Achieving high levels of accuracy in a search result therefore requires an indexing process that considers many more factors for every page of information than the simple presence or absence of the word being searched for. You will remember from chapter 1 that this was one of Google's differentiators at its inception; estimates of the number of factors it uses every time a URL is matched to a particular search expression are in the hundreds, a number that is increasing as Google indexes more and more information from more and more sources. The following chapters cover these factors in more detail, but it is helpful to expand on a few of them here.

When Google indexes a page of content, it doesn't just store the URL against the individual words that appear but also stores it against a list of the phrases that appear. These will be groups of two, three, four, five, etc., words or other strings of characters, such as a model number for a TV. This model number string may appear within a phrase that includes the brand name and other strings of characters that identify the type of TV, such as 'LCD TV'. Such a phrase may easily be made up of six strings of characters, separated by spaces; for example, 'Panasonic 37 inch TX-L37510B LCD TV'. Google will have a list of such six-'word' phrases in its index, against

---

[1] Many computer scientists call this an inverted index, even though it is clearly the right way up.

which there will be list of URLs from all the retail, review and manufacturer sites that have such a phrase in their content.

Google's decisions about which phrases to create index entries for, and which to ignore, of the virtually infinite[1] number of possible phrases that could exist from the vocabulary of the English language (let alone the other languages of the world and the strings of characters that aren't actually words, in any language), will be made with reference to their occurrence in the information Google retrieves from the web, cross-referenced with their occurrence in the long tail of searches users type into Google. This cross-referencing, while still producing an incomprehensibly large – but apparently manageable – number of potential phrases, will nevertheless be a long way short of the actual number of possible phrases, which makes Google's indexing job rather more achievable.

Examples of the sorts of factors Google has decided to consider in its indexing process, particularly when evaluating the Relevance of a page to a word or phrase (and vice versa), include:

- **Existence.** Does the word that is searched for exist in the page?
- **Citation.** Does the word exist in something that links to the page?
  - Where in the source of the link does the word appear?
  - How relevant to that word is the source of the link?
  - How authoritative is the source of the link?

---

[1] To get a sense of the numbers, if there are 250,000 active words in the English language and you were only interested in six-word phrases, it would require every square metre of the land mass on planet Earth to be neck deep in Blu-ray discs just to have enough digital memory to store them. We worked it out.

- **Positioning.** Where is the word located in the text? Near the beginning? Near the end? In headings, subheadings, titles, paragraphs?
- **Relationship.** Are the words related to the main subject of the page? Do other related words exist in the page? For example:
  - Words that mean more or less the same thing (synonyms). 'Tome' is a synonym of 'book'.
  - Words that refer to a more general concept (hypernyms). 'Publication' is a hypernym of 'book'.
  - Words that refer to a more specific concept (hyponyms). 'Paperback', 'novel', 'bible' are all hyponyms of 'book'.
  - Words that refer to things that make up the concept (meronyms). 'Page', 'binding', 'dust-jacket' are all meronyms of 'book'.
  - Words referring to something of which the concept is a part (holonyms). 'Library' is a holonym of 'book'.

Google is particularly keen on things that have sibling relationships (in other words, that share the same hypernym). For example, Google knows that Manchester United, Chelsea and Tottenham Hotspur all refer to the English football clubs. To get a feeling for how good (and bad) Google may be at this in various subject areas, play with Google Sets at http://labs.google.com/sets and Google Squared at http://www.google.com/squared.

- **Proximity.** If more than one word is being searched for, how close together are the words in the page?
- **Co-occurrence**[1]. If more than one word is being searched for, how frequently do these words occur

---

[1] We are not absolutely sure that Google are considering this one. But we're pretty confident.

with other words across the whole document collection? Are they unusual words, or common words? What about the words they occur with?

There are also a few other things that Google can measure about the page itself:

- How natural is the language? Is it grammatically constructed in a way typical of good, authoritative websites? Or does it read like a horrible, spammy website, with repeated keywords scattered throughout the document?
- Is it part of a collection of other documents or pages? If so, are they relevant to the search word(s)? To its related words?
  - How long has the collection been around?
  - How often is the collection updated?
  - How many other places link to it? Are they good, authoritative places?
  - Does the collection link to places that are relevant to the search words? Are they good, authoritative places?
  - Is the collection responsive? Does it load quickly when visited?

These are not the only things Google can consider, but they give you some idea of the job Google is doing to create its index of the world's information. As we have already said, the number of factors Google uses to assess the Relevance of content to particular words is in the hundreds, so this can only be a very brief introduction.

2.6 ASSESSING THE AUTHORITY OF CONTENT

When faced with the millions of pieces of information that Google has worked out are probably relevant to the needs of specific searchers, and which are now sitting happily in its index, its next job is to put them in some sort of order that represents how useful they are likely to be, because in an index this big there are very long lists of URLs that appear to be identically relevant. An assessment of their likely usefulness is needed because this is why people use Google in the first place: they want Google to sort out the mass of stuff on the web so they can find what they're looking for.

Sorting millions of pieces of information into some sort of ranked order by usefulness is clearly a significant task and one that has to be completed automatically and at very great speed in order for Google to continue to please its users. We described earlier the almost incomprehensible scale of Google's index and the masses of queries it receives daily, up to 20% of which it has not seen before: this a computing challenge quite unlike any previously undertaken in the public eye. When we discussed the Wisdom of Crowds, we told you how Google uses the idea that the more people that link to a particular website from their own websites, the more likely the site they are linking to is going to be useful to other people. Well we are now going to analyse this in more detail.

There are three main reasons why Google has chosen a measure that looks at the links that exist between sites as a method to rank the information it finds, and they are:

1. Relevance does not equal usefulness.
2. People lie.
3. Collective wisdom works.

To understand the first point, consider the massively dupli-cated, but highly relevant, use of a manufacturer's description of a single product across multiple retailer websites. There is no way that Google can use identical copies of the same information to rank the different sites by usefulness.

Moving on to the second point: that's right, Google doesn't trust you to only have appropriately relevant information on your website – appropriate, that is, to the services or products you can genuinely provide in a useful way. Why should it, when so many websites clearly exaggerate what they are capable of in the name of marketing differentiation or spamming deceit.

Google's approach to avoiding the untrustworthy and to ranking the relevant is what makes it uniquely powerful, and is at the heart of its success. Its Wisdom of Crowds method taps into the people's appetite for referencing the things that they find useful and interesting by linking to them from their own sites, and the sheer scale of these links – estimates suggest there are trillions – provides a reliable and representative source of 'voting' data to help Google identify the most useful information on the web. So how does Google assess the links that it finds between websites? To answer that question, we're going to ruin our 'links = votes' metaphor.

Although we have referred to the links between sites as democratic judgements, the web is not a real democracy in Google's eyes, because each voting link is not equally influential, unlike the votes in a real democracy. Some sites carry the equivalent of many more votes, and this influence is a critical component of Google's method – it has visited the linking sites and established some key information about them while doing so, information that allows them greater influence. Google's decision-making regarding how influential it will allow sites to be when linking to others is dependent on their Reputation, and the quality and scale of a site's Reputation is a factor of two main considerations:

1. Is the content on the site that is the source of the link relevant to content on the site that is the target of the link?

2. Do sites that, in turn, link to the source site have Reputation of their own?

If the answer is yes to both of these questions the linking site is going to be more influential and carry more authority, which effectively means it gets more votes to pass on to the sites it links to, thereby positively influencing Google's view of the target.

The Power of Anchor Text

A specific part of Google's interest in how a link represents a relevant vote is to do with the judgement the source site makes in its choice of the words used in the construction of the link itself. When a link is constructed, it is done so as HTML and it has two main components: the target URL and the text that represents the link on the source web page, which is called the anchor text. A link looks like this in HTML: **<a href="http://www.bbc.co.uk/">BBC</a>**, where the content in the **<>** brackets is the link code and its URL target, while the letters between them, 'BBC' in this case, is the anchor text. Frequently the creators of links simply use the URL target itself as the anchor, particularly if it is to the main web address of the target site – which in this case would be www.bbc.co.uk – but when the target of the link is a more specific piece of content, the person constructing the link is likely to distil an essence of what the content is about into a few words and put them into the anchor text. Such a decision achieves two main things: the web visitor who sees the text gets a helpful micro-summary of the content of the target page, and Google, when it crawls the source page, finds a democratic judgement in the form of a few words, carefully chosen by a human being, about the subject of the target page. Google has decided that this carefully chosen distillation of the content of the target web page is hugely valuable in its assessment of the Relevance that target page has to those few words when they subsequently appear in a search. Anchor text is one of the most powerful factors in Google's usefulness armoury.

It's hard to imagine the recursive assessments Google applies to all the interlinking sites going back and back up the chain of links, calculating their ability to improve the Reputation of the sites they link to, but this is the principle at play here. Google's massive computing power is churning through these two main calculations of Relevance – of the content itself to the searches being made – and Reputation – the combination of the Relevance and authority of the linking sites – in order to ensure that the sites in its results for any search are not only relevant but are also ranked by usefulness.

Despite the many words employed in this chapter so far, the topics covered are just a small number of the factors at work in Google's indexing process. We believe, however, that they are some of the most significant, at least conceptually, and it is our ambition in the rest of this book to make sense of enough of the factors to give you the confidence to change your site in ways that will cause Google to love it more. Google's love is a hard love and its indexing processes are profoundly complex and difficult to pick apart. But we do know enough about the principles to help you in a practical way to build a better website that is more deserving of Google's love.

Before we move on to the more practical stuff, we need to spend a bit of time looking at actual search behaviour and what Google does with the words users type into its unassuming interface.

2.7 UNDERSTANDING SEARCHES

Earlier, in section 1.2 Organising the World's Information, we referred to the hundreds of millions of different things that are typed into Google every day as a huge and remarkable window into people's souls. Google's use of this stream of humankind's consciousness is, fortunately, 'Not Evil'[1]. Google uses this window to understand its users' needs better and to improve their access to the part of the world's information it has already organised. Sometimes this job is relatively easy – when the intention of a search is clear and unambiguous – while at other times it is more difficult and Google has to work harder to present searchers with results that match its perception of their needs.

When we look closely at an example of an ambiguous search, the effort that Google routinely extends to understand what is wanted becomes clearer. With a simple search for the word 'apple', Google's understanding of the searcher's need is limited because there is more than one possible meaning of the word 'apple' in the context of a search of the world's information. Google has to make a number of primary judgements to clear up this ambiguity and they begin with clarifying the likely relationship the search term has with other information that might satisfy the searcher's need. On one level Google can use the indexing model described in the previous section to compare the indexed information it has for the word 'apple' and offer up the URLs it considers useful. As the data grows, however, this technique on its own is insufficient because it is possible that the information it has already organised into its index could be skewed in its volume and apparent usefulness and not be representative of the fundamental need a searcher may have. Such a possible skew is particularly clear in the 'apple' example, where for the vast majority of the documented

---

[1] No. 6 in Google's Philosophy: You can make money without doing evil (see http://www.google.com/corporate/tenthings.html).

history of humankind the word 'apple' has chiefly meant a fruit, specifically the pomaceous fruit of the tree *Malus domestica*. However, for the snapshot of the last 30 years which overlaps neatly with the birth and maturing of computerised information retrieval, 'apple' has developed a powerful secondary meaning as the brand name of a large computing and consumer electronics manufacturer. And on the web, in the early 21st century, this secondary meaning has thoroughly overtaken the original. Nothing makes this clearer than comparing a search for the singular and plural versions of 'apple' on Google.

Apple (United Kingdom)
Apple designs and creates iPod and iTunes, Mac laptop and desktop computers, the OS X operating system, and the revolutionary iPhone.
www.apple.com/uk/ - Cached - Similar

iPhone   Downloads
iPod touch   Support
Mac   iPod nano
iPod + iTunes   Store
More results from apple.com »

Apple - iPhone - Mobile phone, iPod, and Internet device.
iPhone 3GS is a GSM cell phone that's also an iPod, a video camera, and a mobile Internet device with email and GPS maps.
www.apple.com/iphone/ - Cached - Similar

Welcome to the Apple Store - Apple Store (U.K.)
Available exclusively from Apple Online and Apple Retail Store. ... You can also order from The Apple Store by calling 0800 048 0408. ...
store.apple.com/uk - Cached - Similar

Welcome to the Apple Store - Apple Store (U.S.)
Experience the wide world of Apple at the Apple Store. Shop for Apple computers, iPod and iPhone models, and discover Apple and third-party ...
store.apple.com/ - United States - Cached - Similar
⊞ Show more results from store.apple.com

News results for apple
Apple admits using child labour to build iPods and iPhones in ... - 3 hours ago
By Daily Mail Reporter Technology giant Apple has admitted that child labour has been employed at some of the factories that build its iPods, computers and ...
Daily Mail - 13 related articles »
Apple's Bikini Ban: A Developer's Story - PC World - 27 related articles »
Jobs: I'll decide what to do with Apple's $40bn cash pile -
Register - 475 related articles »

Apple Illustration
Welcome to the Apple Agency website. You will find a multitude of illustrations which have been commissioned from agencies & clients throughout the world. ...
www.apple.co.uk/ - Cached - Similar

Apple - Wikipedia, the free encyclopedia
There are more than 7500 known cultivars of apples resulting in a range of ... English scholar H. R. Ellis Davidson links apples to religious practices in ...
Botanical information - History - Cultural aspects - Apple cultivars
en.wikipedia.org/wiki/Apple - Cached - Similar

Apple Inc. - Wikipedia, the free encyclopedia
The Apple I, Apple's first product. Sold as an assembled circuit board, ... The Macintosh Portable was Apple's first "portable" Macintosh computer, ...
en.wikipedia.org/wiki/Apple_Inc. - Cached - Similar

Apple (United Kingdom)
Apple designs and creates iPod and iTunes, Mac laptop and desktop computers, the OS X operating system, and the revolutionary iPhone.
www.apple.com/uk/ - Cached - Similar

Apple - iPhone - Mobile phone, iPod, and Internet device.
iPhone 3GS is a GSM cell phone that's also an iPod, a video camera, and a mobile Internet device with email and GPS maps.
www.apple.com/iphone/ - United States - Cached - Similar
⊞ Show more results from www.apple.com

Image results for apples - Report images

WHFoods: Apples
A link that takes you to the In-Depth Nutritional Profile for Apples, ... Whole apples are a much better nutritional choice than apple juice. ...
www.whfoods.com/genpage.php?dbid=15&tname ... - Cached - Similar

Apples - descriptions, flavours, apple trees for sale, apple ...
If you want to discuss apple varieties, apple flavours, orchards, and how different apple varieties are related, you have come to the right place! ...
www.orangepippin.com/ - Cached - Similar

Apples - Google Books Result
Roger Yepsen - 1996 - Cooking - 255 pages
Ninety North American apples, described in words and identified in the author's beautiful and precise watercolors.In this charming and informative book, Roger ...
books.google.co.uk/books?isbn=0393115673...

To attempt to accommodate such bias in the information Google has already organised, it supplements its existing usefulness assessment with insight it draws from the stream of search behaviour. It does this by looking at the presence of other words that may appear alongside 'apple' when they are searched in combination. Among this data it finds a very wide variety of searches that include things like 'apple ipod', 'apple computers', 'apple records', 'apple pie recipe' and 'fiona apple', but with widely varying volumes of searches for each. Google can clarify the likely intention of the searcher by cross-referencing its current assessment of the most useful URLs in its index for the word 'apple', with a probability that the searcher has a particular intent in mind, by analysing these varying volumes. The higher the volume of searches for 'apple ipod' compared to other terms including 'apple', such as 'apple records', the higher the likelihood that the intention behind a search for 'apple' is for the brand manufacturer of the iPod and not the Beatles' record company or the fruit. The analysis of these additional search terms goes a long way to clarify the likely intent of the searcher, as does a careful evaluation of the intent when the same words are present in a search but in a different order; for example, 'dog bites man' does not have the same meaning as 'man bites dog', nor is 'apple records' the same as 'recording on an apple mac'. Despite all this analysis Google is still playing a game of probability, because it cannot know the intent of the searcher, so it has to make a guess, and even after its best efforts with the 'apple' search there will still be plenty of searchers who actually wanted information about the fruit, but didn't get it.

Google's response to this continuing challenge is to take its probability assessments a step further still. Nothing speaks to Google louder on subject of intent than a user's behaviour. The Wisdom of Crowds is predicated on this – the behaviour of 'voting' for a page of content by linking to it across the web – and there is a pool of additional behaviours that Google can analyse to interpret likely intent. They look at what searchers do after they are presented with the results of Google's first best guess – the first set of ten ranked results for a particular search. Remember, Google is fanatical about the relevance of its results and the satisfaction of its users, so if it can learn from them what they thought of the results it presented, it will. Google analyses very carefully three main behaviours following the presentation of a set of results: which specific result is clicked on; how long the searcher was away from the results before clicking on another result; and how the search was subsequently refined. Taking these in turn, let's examine what Google learns from such analysis.

1. Google knows which result a searcher clicks on by redirecting every click from its results page through a tracking mechanism. This choice is recorded as a simple form of positive vote for the URL clicked on, which Google then allows to improve the URL's usefulness score for that specific search phrase. A click on a result for www.apple.com therefore improves its chances of being ranked highly in subsequent searches for 'apple'.

2. Google assumes that if a click on another result from the same set of results happens quite soon after the previous click, it amounts to a negative vote for the first page visited. The assumption is that the page wasn't as useful to the searcher as Google originally thought it was. A click on a result for the home page of 'Apple Records' that was shortly followed by a click from the same set of results for a page about 'How Apple Records Music'[1] will reduce Google's view of the usefulness of the Apple Records website to searches that include the phrase 'Apple Records'.

3. Google tracks carefully how a search is refined, namely by the addition or removal of words searched for following a previous search. Google uses these refinements to build on its understanding of the relationship between words and their likely patterns of intent. A refinement that added the word 'crumble' to an 'apple' search will shift Google's perception of the likely intent of the original search for 'apple' towards recipes that include the fruit and away from the brand manufacturer.

---

[1] This is notionally a page from the apple.com website about the technology behind music recording on Apple Macs, but it is a fiction for the sake of this example.

The individual visits and changes a single user makes are not going to have a perceptible effect on Google's assessments of usefulness, but when the scale of such actions on a daily basis across Google's network of search websites is factored in, it represents another aspect of the crowd-wisdom concept that can help Google. Daily use of Google, therefore, includes a constant flow of voting and refining that is immensely valuable to Google and its ongoing challenge of returning useful results to our searches.

At a basic level Google's mission is to provide people with answers to their needs. While the exact expression of that need, insofar as Google can infer it from the characters and words typed in, is often enough to get Google close to an answer, the ever-improving software at the heart of its engine seeks better and better clarification and more and more accurate refinement as the scale of the information increases and the breadth of people's needs finds greater expression online.

2.8 THE PRINCIPLES OF GOOGLE'S LOVE

Google's processes and methods for assessing the likely usefulness of websites – the things that underpin its inclination to love a website or not – can be separated into three groups: those that help Google find and interpret the structure of information; those that help Google understand the meaning of information; and those that help Google assess the authority of the information it has found and understood. These principles have been discussed in the previous sections, but now it's time to bring them together so that you can grasp the whole picture.

2.8.1 Visibility

Google has to find the world's information before it can index it and present it within its results. This requires websites to be visible to Google's software and the information available to be well organised and structured for machine processing. We refer to this principle as 'Visibility'.

2.8.2 Relevance

The next step is to decide what the world's information is actually about and whether any part of it matches the things people search for. Google's pursuit of the meaning of information and its efforts to match it with the searches people make is at the heart of its decisions about whether a site is relevant or not to the needs of users. We refer to this principle as 'Relevance'.

2.8.3 Reputation

Finally, faced with multiple sources of apparently meaningful information, Google has to decide which are the most authoritative, or trustworthy. Comparing the quality and quantity of the references these sources have from around the web enables Google to assess the Reputation of the information and rank it by likely usefulness in its results. Unsurprisingly, we refer to this principle as 'Reputation'.

Google's love for a site is therefore an amalgam of the site's Visibility, Relevance and Reputation. A highly visible, well-organised website full of information that is deeply relevant to the demands of its customers, and valued by a community of relevant websites who happily link to it, is a recipe for profound and long-lasting love from Google. And such love has a very powerful side-effect – one that your consumption of this book proves you are very keen to acquire – lots of visitors who are interested in what you have to say or sell!

To fix these principles in your mind we have created a simple conceptual model of them and what they support. The principles of Visibility, Relevance and Reputation support the performance of a website in the non-sponsored, non-paid and, therefore, free search results in the main body of the Google results page. We call these the natural search results, but they are also referred to as organic search results. The opposites of 'natural' and 'organic' results are the 'manufactured', 'genetically modified' results for which Google has a whole bunch of other rules to determine their ranking. Those paid results are not our concern right now, because you are about to meet the Tripod of Love.

2.9 THE TRIPOD OF LOVE: VISIBILITY, RELEVANCE AND REPUTATION

The Tripod of Love is our visual metaphor for how Google's love, and hence the high performance of your website in its natural search results, sits upon a tripod that is supported by the three legs of Visibility, Relevance and Reputation. A tripod is a three-legged object, generally one used as a platform of some sort, which is not a job that can be done very well by anything with fewer legs. Google's love for your site is therefore utterly dependent on your supporting it with three robust legs of Visibility, Relevance and Reputation. How you go about building these legs and lifting your site up onto this platform – whether a new or existing website – is what we get on to next.

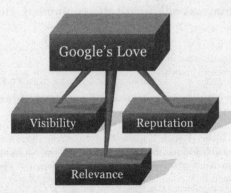

Illustration 2: The Tripod of Love: Visibility, Relevance and Reputation in support of Google's love and natural search performance

2.10 CHAPTER FOOTNOTE: GOOGLE AND THE BAG OF LOVE

We were reluctant to explore the PageRank equation earlier in this chapter, but we cannot resist an attempt to illustrate what it means, now you've read the sections about Reputation. It is not critical that you read this, but it may help you grasp more of the meaning in it. We reckon you are ready for it now.

When thinking about the love Google has to offer websites, imagine it having two large bags of love. One bag contains Reputation love, the other bag contains Relevance love.

The bag of love of Relevance is shared out between all the pages on the web based on the existence of words from the search query and on a host of other considerations: structural information, word position and more[1].

The bag of love of Reputation is different: it is shared out in a dance[2]. To begin the dance, Google shares out all the love in the bag of Reputation between all the pages it has found on the web[3]. Then the dance steps commence. At each step, every page shares out all the love it has between all the pages it links to. It then in turn receives a share of love from all the pages that link to it.

Some random acts of love are also committed. Here, instead

---

[1] Which you will learn about in the following chapters.

[2] You will see references elsewhere to the Google dance – the periodic fluctuations in rank caused by an update to Google's list of Reputation love. We have unapologetically stolen the term and beaten it into a highly stretched metaphor. It's almost translucent if you hold it up to the light.

[3] The amount of love received by each page in this initial sharing of love depends on a number of factors. Google is naturally pretty cagey about what exactly they are, but they probably include the form and length of anchor text pointing to the page, the location of links to the page in the pages pointing to it, and the similarity of content between linkers and linkees. Another powerful way of refining the initial shares would be to know where real people go on web pages and adjust the shares according to the numbers of visitors. We suggest that this may be why Google Analytics is free.

of a share of love being passed along a link, it is given to another randomly chosen page[1]. This stops love piling up on pages that do not pass it along, it keeps things interesting, and ensures an elegant dance.

The dance stops when a new step no longer changes the amount of love each dancer holds – in other words when the love each page receives equals the love it gave in the last step[2]. The love held by each page is recorded in what might be called the list of love.

The dance can be written in matrix maths notation as:

$$\pi^T = \pi^T(\alpha S + (1-\alpha)E)$$

This is Google's PageRank equation as introduced at the beginning of this chapter.

In our way of thinking, π^T is Google's list of the Reputation love held by every page on the web. In the dance itself, $\alpha S + (1-\alpha)E$, α is Google's boredom threshold – its predilection to passing love along a page's links (which it does about 85% of the time), as opposed to committing random acts of love ($1-\alpha$, or about 15% of the time). S is the matrix describing the love passed from every page on the web to every other page in the web. E is the matrix describing the random acts of love committed between every page on the web and every other page on the web.

We believe that this attempt to bring the maths down to earth is important for the more adventurous reader, because the simplistic view of the flow of Reputation quickly hits some conceptual buffers. At least with this 'bag of love' metaphor you may be a little happier with it as a process.

---

[1] Not evenly. Google may tweak the probability of spreading the love depending on topic or user type.

[2] The length of time that this will take depends on Google's boredom threshold – some very clever people believe it to be the 142nd step.

50 WAYS . . .

1. Always refer to The Tripod of Love: Visibility, Relevance and Reputation when working to improve Google's love for your website. *See section 2.9*

3

CREATE YOUR WEBSITE FOR YOUR USERS

If you are reading this chapter straight after chapter 2, you need to hold onto that image of the Tripod of Love, as everything you do or read from this point on will be in support of one of the three principles of Visibility, Relevance and Reputation. If you haven't read chapter 2, then sorry, but you really must head back there now; it is simply too important to skip.

Google's approach to its mission requires it first to actually find the content out there on the web, so we should naturally talk about Visibility first when discussing how Google works. However, building a website that is worthy of Google's love does not start with how to build it technically: it starts with what you put on it and how that relates to the needs of your customers or visitors – in other words, its Relevance to your market. Building a website that is as relevant as it possibly can be to the needs of your visitors – as they express them, not as you perceive them – will give you the best possible start in Google's eyes. This chapter is therefore focused on building the best possible Relevance support for the natural search performance of your site.

3.1 BUILDING RELEVANCE: WHAT DO PEOPLE WANT?

There is a design movement on the web that believes the primary aim of website design should be to serve the goals of the users of the site. This may not sound very controversial, but think for a minute how you might answer the following questions about your website:

- What colour should it be?
- How should it be laid out?
- What should we name our products or services?
- How should we divide up the material on our site?
- What should we write about?

We believe that the correct answer to every one of these questions is:

I don't really know.

This is the central premise of what is known as 'user-centred design'. Every design decision should be referred back to what we know about the users of the site, not simply to the beliefs, prejudices or even brilliant insights of the site owner or the site's designer.

You, of course, know a lot about the subject matter of your site – more than the likely users of your site ever will, no doubt. And we're not saying that your goals are not important – they are. But in this user-centred world you can only pursue your goals through supporting the goals your users have, because your users don't start on your home page. They start at Google[1]. And they type in a query that reflects their goal. The pages that Google returns will be those that Google believes supports that goal, namely the most 'useful' pages it can find. And if they arrive on your site and do not immediately see something that suggests their goal will be supported, they will leave. The web, as they say, is a pull medium, not a push medium. The power is

---

[1] Admittedly, not all of them do. If you are lucky enough to have a well-recognised brand, then many will find you through that (even if this means just typing your brand name into Google). But for most sites, the vast majority of visitors will have found you originally via Google. In fact, if you have any web analytics set up on your site, why not go right now and find out what percentage of your new visitors come from Google. If you don't have this information to hand, we suggest that you assume it's above 50%.

with the user, not the site owner, and that's why it's more important to design for their goals than for yours.

There are a number of ways in which you can investigate what it is that people really want from you. You can ask several thousand people a few questions (such as in a market research questionnaire). You can ask a few people a lot of questions (such as in a user goals study or a focus group). Or you can check what millions of people express as their goals, to Google. We would argue that the last of these is the most critical for a website – to match what you offer to the way people ask Google for it.

Let's examine how you can make sure that the ways in which you describe what you are offering match the ways in which people ask Google for them.

3.2 BASIC SEARCH DEMAND ANALYSIS

Bob, owner of Bob's Goldfish Emporium[1], wants to start marketing his goldfish online. He is using google.co.uk to investigate how his product is described. Firstly, he types in 'goldfish'.

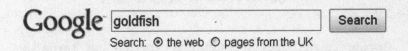

Google returns a mixed bag of results, including a credit card brand, a Wikipedia entry, a fish pet shop, an advice page, some videos, an art gallery, and a couple of news stories. Bob then looks to the bottom of the page, where he sees:

---

[1] We made up Bob. If your name is Bob, and you do own a Goldfish Emporium, apologies for the bizarre coincidence. We couldn't find you on Google. On the plus side, you're about to read a chapter that's very relevant to your business.

Searches related to: **goldfish**

goldfish **care**	**pet** goldfish	**looking after** goldfish	**keeping** goldfish
goldfish **types**	goldfish **breeding**	goldfish **diseases**	goldfish **illness**

Bob notes down each of the related searches for later.

Next, Bob decides to see what else people are calling goldfish. He decides to try using Google's 'synonym' operator, the '~' (the tilde). In mathematical notation, '~' means 'is equivalent to' or 'is similar to'. On your keyboard, the tilde is usually to be found by holding down the shift key and pressing the '#' key (look on the right hand side of your keyboard, just to the left of the enter key, and below the ']' key)[1]. Bob knows that if you use a tilde in front of a word that you type into Google, such as '~run', Google will return pages that contain not only that word but also words that are similar in meaning, such as runner, runners, running and marathon. Google tends to refer to these as 'synonyms'.

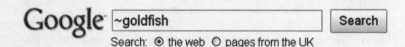

Google returns pages on goldfish, as expected, but also on koi carp. Now Bob knows full well that koi carp aren't goldfish; however, they are related. You can mate a goldfish with a koi and they will produce offspring, but sterile ones – just like horses and donkeys. Nevertheless, it's clear that, as far as Google is concerned, koi and goldfish are synonyms. Bob notes down 'koi' for further investigation. He checks the related searches, and notes them down too:

---

[1] On American, Australian and Canadian keyboard layouts, hold down the shift key and press the ' ` ' key, at the top left corner of the keyboard.

Searches related to: **~goldfish**

koi goldfish   koi carp   koi for sale   koi ponds

shubunkin goldfish   sanke koi   japanese koi   koi varieties

Bob now uses another operator, '-' (the dash) to exclude the word 'goldfish' from the results; think of it as a minus sign.

Google   ~goldfish -goldfish   Search
Search: ⦿ the web ◯ pages from the UK

Google returns lots more results for 'koi', as well as some more related searches:

Searches related to: **~goldfish -goldfish**

japanese koi   koi pond pumps   koi for sale   koi varieties

sanke koi   koi nishikigoi   kohaku koi   koi fish

There are a few repeated terms here, so Bob notes down the new ones.

Google has returned a lot of koi-related results, but Bob can't see any others, so he excludes 'koi' from his search too.

Google   ~goldfish -goldfish -koi   Search
Search: ⦿ the web ◯ pages from the UK

Google now returns pages with the two-word phrase 'gold fish'. Interesting. Bob had forgotten that some people would write it as two separate words. He writes 'gold fish' on his list and adds 'gold-fish' too, just in case. He also looks at the related searches:

Searches related to: **~goldfish -goldfish -koi**

goldfish fish tank   **goldfish aquarium**   **goldfish swimming**   **eat goldfish**
goldfish stress

Bob notes them down too. 'Eat goldfish'? What is wrong with these people?

Google | ~goldfish -goldfish -koi -"gold fish" | **Search**
Search: ⊙ the web ○ pages from the UK

Bob then has one more go, this time excluding 'gold fish' too. But the results seem irrelevant to his offering, so he ignores them. The related searches are still interesting, so he notes them down.

Searches related to: **~goldfish -goldfish -koi -"gold fish"**

fisherman goldfish   **fishing goldfish**   **freshwater goldfish**   **goldfish saltwater**
goldfish tanks   **fat goldfish**   **rare goldfish**

Bob looks at his list so far:

1. goldfish
2. goldfish care
3. pet goldfish
4. looking after goldfish
5. keeping goldfish
6. goldfish types
7. goldfish breeding
8. goldfish diseases
9. goldfish illness
10. koi
11. koi goldfish
12. koi carp
13. koi for sale
14. koi ponds
15. shubunkin goldfish
16. sanke koi
17. koi varieties
18. japanese koi
19. koi pond pumps
20. koi nishikigoi

21. kohaku koi
22. koi fish
23. goldfish fish tank
24. goldfish aquarium
25. goldfish swimming
26. eat goldfish
27. goldfish stress
28. gold fish

29. gold-fish
30. fisherman goldfish
31. fishing goldfish
32. freshwater goldfish
33. goldfish saltwater
34. goldfish tanks
35. fat goldfish
36. rare goldfish

Bob now has a list of search terms to investigate.

3.3 THE GOOGLE KEYWORD TOOL

Bob looks at his list of words. He knows that people are searching for these terms, but how many people? Time to ask a few more questions of Google. Bob finds the Google Keyword Tool at https://adwords.google.com/select/KeywordToolExternal[1].

---

[1] We have asked Google if this URL is a permanent one; they couldn't promise that it is, so please accept our apologies if they have moved or changed the Keyword Tool since this book was published.

Note the line 'Results are tailored to **English, United States**'. These are the default settings, but Bob is interested in the UK market (goldfish are hard to ship internationally), so he clicks the blue 'Edit' link beside it and selects 'English, United Kingdom'.

To start with, he types in just one word: 'goldfish'. He leaves 'Use Synonyms' checked – no point in excluding them. He then types in the characters he sees in the picture, to prove to Google that he's a human being, not a computer program. Then he presses the 'Get keyword ideas' button.

Using the 'Choose columns to be displayed' dropdown select box, Bob hides the Global Monthly Search Volume and shows the Search Volume Trends.

Choose columns to be displayed: ⑦
Show/hide columns

Keywords	Advertiser Competition ⑦	Local Search Volume: September ⑦	Search Volume Trends (Oct 2008 - Sep 2009) ⑦	Match Type: ⑦ Broad ▼
Keywords related to term(s) entered - sorted by relevance ⑦				
goldfish care		5,400		Add ≽
fancy goldfish		5,400		Add ≽
shubunkin goldfish		590		Add ≽
goldfish tank		14,800		Add ≽
goldfish		368,000		Add ≽
goldfish bowl		22,200		Add ≽
ranchu goldfish		390		Add ≽
goldfish varieties		Not enough data	No data	Add ≽
oranda goldfish		1,300		Add ≽
breeding goldfish		1,900		Add ≽
comet goldfish		1,300		Add ≽
goldfish feeding		1,300		Add ≽
goldfish food		4,400		Add ≽
goldfish aquarium		4,400		Add ≽
goldfish crackers		590		Add ≽
goldfish types		Not enough data	No data	Add ≽
goldfish temperature		Not enough data	No data	Add ≽
red goldfish		2,400		Add ≽
goldfish tail		Not enough data	No data	Add ≽
goldfish diseases		4,400		Add ≽
koi goldfish		1,300		Add ≽
calico goldfish		Not enough data	No data	Add ≽
goldfish fry		Not enough data	No data	Add ≽
small goldfish		1,300		Add ≽
lionhead goldfish		720		Add ≽
fantail goldfish		4,400		Add ≽
goldfish ponds		720		Add ≽
bubble eye goldfish		590		Add ≽
pond goldfish		5,400		Add ≽
goldfish aquariums		480		Add ≽
blue goldfish		720		Add ≽

He notices a few things immediately. Firstly, there are hundreds of thousands of people searching for goldfish online. This is reassuring, as he was wondering whether there was a strong online marketplace.

Secondly, Bob notes that these phrases are currently 'sorted by relevance' and that the search term he entered is not considered the most relevant, which is very interesting and clearly worthy of some further investigation. As far as Google is concerned, the things that it expects to find in content relating to goldfish include 'goldfish care' and 'fancy goldfish' – which a lot of people search for – as well as the far less frequently searched-for phrases 'shubunkin goldfish' and 'ranchu goldfish'. Google considers these terms as signifying content related to goldfish – which makes sense, as any website that mentions them is pretty definitely highly goldfish-related – and Bob decides that he will write about them on his site to demonstrate his goldfish expertise to Google, even if not many people are searching for them.

Thirdly, some trends can be spotted. For example, searches for 'ranchu goldfish' have grown steadily over the last year. It doesn't look seasonal; if it were, you would expect the bars for Oct 08 and Sep 09 to be of similar heights. He resolves to chat to some friends in the industry about whether they are detecting increasing demand for 'ranchu goldfish', and perhaps consider sourcing some as a new product – a little speculative, but an article and some photos on the site will soon show him if people are interested, simply by whether or not they read it[1].

Next, Bob clicks the blue column heading 'Local Search Volume', which sorts the list by search volume.

---

[1] Bob is going to put Google Analytics on his site precisely so he can keep an eye on this kind of stuff.

| | | | Choose columns to be displayed: ⑦ | |
| | | | Show/hide columns ▾ | |
Keywords	Advertiser Competition ⑦	▼ Local Search Volume: September ⑦	Search Volume Trends (Oct 2008 - Sep 2009) ⑦	Match Type: ⑦ Broad ▾
Keywords related to term(s) entered - sort by relevance ⑦				
goldfish	▰▰	368,000	▂▅█████████	Add ≫
goldfish bowl	▰	22,200	▂▃▅███████	Add ≫
goldfish tank	▰	14,800	▂▅███████	Add ≫
black goldfish	▰	6,600	▃▅██████	Add ≫
goldfish fish	▰	6,600	▂▃▅██████	Add ≫
fancy goldfish	▰	5,400	▃▅██████	Add ≫
goldfish bowls	▰	5,400	▂▅██████	Add ≫
goldfish care	▰	5,400	▂▅██████	Add ≫
pond goldfish	▰	5,400	▃▅██████	Add ≫
fantail goldfish	▰	4,400	▂▅██████	Add ≫
goldfish aquarium	▰	4,400	▂▅██████	Add ≫
goldfish diseases	▰	4,400	▂▅██████	Add ≫
goldfish food	▰	4,400	▂▅██████	Add ≫
goldfish live	▰	4,400	▃▅██████	Add ≫
goldfish tanks	▰	4,400	▂▅██████	Add ≫
pet goldfish	▰	4,400	▂▅██████	Add ≫
goldfish water	▰	3,600	▂▅██████	Add ≫
pregnant goldfish	▰	3,600	▂▅██████	Add ≫
buy" goldfish	▱	2,900	▂▅██████	Add ≫
goldfish glass	▰	2,900	▂▅██████	Add ≫
goldfish pictures	▰	2,400	▃▅██████	Add ≫
red goldfish	▰	2,400	▂▅██████	Add ≫
breeding goldfish	▰	1,900	▂▅██████	Add ≫
feed goldfish	▰	1,600	▂▅██████	Add ≫
black moor goldfish	▰	1,300	▂▅██████	Add ≫
comet goldfish	▰	1,300	▂▅██████	Add ≫
goldfish feeding	▰	1,300	▂▅██████	Add ≫
koi goldfish	▰	1,300	▃▅██████	Add ≫
moor goldfish	▰	1,300	▃▅██████	Add ≫
oranda goldfish	▰	1,300	▃▅██████	Add ≫
small goldfish	▰	1,300	▃▅██████	Add ≫
types of goldfish	▰	1,300	▂▅██████	Add ≫

He notices that 'goldfish diseases' only appears in the plural, so he'll make sure that a website article on the subject is titled with the plural – 'Goldfish Diseases, Diagnosing and Treating' seems about right – but will mention it in the singular within the article just in case.

At the bottom of the list, Google puts an option to 'Download all keywords: text, .csv (for excel), .csv'. Bob downloads all the terms into a format that Microsoft's Excel spreadsheet program can read, for later perusal.

Bob looks at the 'Match Type:' dropdown select box at the top right of the table. 'Broad' is selected. He changes the selection to

'Exact'[1]. Suddenly, the numbers for 'Local Search volume' are much lower.

Keywords	Advertiser Competition ⑦	▼ Local Search Volume: September ⑦	Search Volume Trends (Oct 2008 - Sep 2009) ⑦	Match Type: ⑦ Exact ▼
Keywords related to term(s) entered - sort by relevance ⑦				
[goldfish]		60,500		Add Exact ⯆
[goldfish bowl]		9,900		Add Exact ⯆
[goldfish diseases]		3,600		Add Exact ⯆
[goldfish care]		2,900		Add Exact ⯆
[goldfish tank]		2,900		Add Exact ⯆
[fancy goldfish]		2,400		Add Exact ⯆
[goldfish bowls]		2,400		Add Exact ⯆
[goldfish tanks]		2,400		Add Exact ⯆
[fantail goldfish]		1,600		Add Exact ⯆
[goldfish food]		1,300		Add Exact ⯆
[pregnant goldfish]		1,300		Add Exact ⯆
[goldfish aquarium]		1,000		Add Exact ⯆
[goldfish types]		1,000		Add Exact ⯆
[types of goldfish]		880		Add Exact ⯆
[black goldfish]		720		Add Exact ⯆
[black moor goldfish]		720		Add Exact ⯆
[buy" goldfish]		590		Add Exact ⯆
[comet goldfish]		590		Add Exact ⯆
[oranda goldfish]		590		Add Exact ⯆
[breeding goldfish]		480		Add Exact ⯆
[goldfish pictures]		480		Add Exact ⯆
[lionhead goldfish]		480		Add Exact ⯆
[pond goldfish]		480		Add Exact ⯆
[goldfish crackers]		390		Add Exact ⯆
[goldfish fish]		390		Add Exact ⯆
[pet goldfish]		390		Add Exact ⯆
[sick goldfish]		390		Add Exact ⯆
[bubble eye goldfish]		320		Add Exact ⯆
[goldfish disease]		320		Add Exact ⯆
[goldfish health]		320		Add Exact ⯆
[goldfish illnesses]		320		Add Exact ⯆
[how to breed goldfish]		320		Add Exact ⯆

The previous volume for 'goldfish' – 368,000 – included all searches that contained the word 'goldfish' somewhere within them. Of course, this was just an estimate, but in the absence of

---

[1] Google describes its keyword matching types as follows: Broad includes the volume for searches with similar phrases and relevant variations that include the keyword or phrase. Exact includes only the volume for the exact keyword or phrase. For further details: https://adwords.google.com./support/aw/bin/answer. p1?hl=en-uk&answer=6324.

anything better Bob could only conclude that 368,000 was the total number of people who were asking Google for anything about goldfish. *Anything*. Not potential purchasers – this was everybody. In fact, not even that – this was every question. How many searches might a person who made one search about goldfish make across a month? Five? Yikes. Perhaps only 73,600 people are interested each month. So how many people are actually trying to *buy* goldfish?

Bob tries a broad match search for 'buy goldfish'.

Keywords	Advertiser Competition ⑦	▼ Local Search Volume: September ⑦	Search Volume Trends (Oct 2008 - Sep 2009) ⑦	Match Type: ⑦ Broad ✔
Keywords related to term(s) entered - sort by relevance ⑦				
buy goldfish	▬▬	2,900	▄▅▅▆▇▆▅▆▇▇	Add ⌄
buy goldfish bowl	▬	210	▃▂▃▃▄▇▃▃▃▃	Add ⌄
buy fancy goldfish	▬	91	▁▁▃▁▁▄▃▁▃▁	Add ⌄
buy a goldfish bowl	☐	Not enough data	No data	Add ⌄
buy fancy goldfish online	▬	Not enough data	No data	Add ⌄
buy goldfish bowls	▬	Not enough data	No data	Add ⌄
buy goldfish for	▬	Not enough data	No data	Add ⌄
buy goldfish in	▬	Not enough data	No data	Add ⌄
buy goldfish online	▬▬	Not enough data	No data	Add ⌄
buy goldfish online uk	☐	Not enough data	No data	Add ⌄
buy goldfish pet shop	▬	Not enough data	No data	Add ⌄
buy goldfish pet store	▬	Not enough data	No data	Add ⌄
buy goldfish tank	▬	Not enough data	No data	Add ⌄
buy goldfish uk	▬	Not enough data	No data	Add ⌄
buy live goldfish	▬	Not enough data	No data	Add ⌄
buy pet goldfish	▬	Not enough data	No data	Add ⌄
places to buy goldfish	☐	Not enough data	No data	Add ⌄
to buy goldfish	☐	Not enough data	No data	Add ⌄
where can i buy goldfish	▬	Not enough data	No data	Add ⌄
where to buy goldfish	▬	Not enough data	No data	Add ⌄

Choose columns to be displayed: ⑦
Show/hide columns

Add all 20 »
Download all keywords: text, .csv (for excel), .csv

The result does not look very good: fewer than 3,000 in the whole of the UK. Is that all there are? Well, perhaps not. Bob knows that people looking to purchase often just type in the name of the thing they are looking for, without adding the word 'buy' to it. Bob decides to see if anyone has done any research into this.

They have. Not quite as much, or quite as robust research as Bob would like (the searches analysed weren't typed into Google, they were typed into smaller search engines), but the best estimate he can find comes from a study called *Determining the User Intent of Web Search Engine Queries*[1]. It suggests that 80% of all searches are 'informational' in nature (to find information assumed to be available on the web to read, or links to that information), with a further 10% being 'navigational' (to reach a particular site that the user has in mind, either because they have visited it in the past or because they assume that such a site exists) and the remaining 10% being 'transactional' (looking for a site where further interaction will happen, such as shopping, downloading, database access). Not perfect, but an acceptable rule of thumb.

So where does that leave the online goldfish market sales? Well, 10% of 73,600 searches that include the word 'goldfish' is 7,360 per month. Online goldfish may not be the route to riches he has hoped.

Next up, koi. Again, Bob inputs this as a single word. He leaves the other settings as before.

Here he sees that there is a clear seasonal trend in searches for the majority of koi-related queries. Bob would expect to see a dip over the winter months, and certainly searches for 'koi food' and 'koi for sale' in particular reflect this, with a very clear curve downwards across October to February. Bob also notes that search volumes for 'koi' are over twice as high as those for 'goldfish'. A quick check of the exact match figures doesn't bear this out – 60,500 searches in a month for 'koi', which is the same as the exact match for 'goldfish'. This finding suggests that

[1] Bernard J. Jansen and Danielle L. Booth of Pennsylvania State University, and Amanda Spink of the Queensland University of Technology, http://www2007.org/posters/poster989.pdf

Keywords	Advertiser Competition ?	▼ Local Search Volume: September ?	Search Volume Trends (Oct 2008 - Sep 2009) ?	Match Type: ? Broad
Choose columns to be displayed: ? Show/hide columns				
Keywords related to term(s) entered - sort by relevance ?				
koi		823,000		Add ≈
koi carp		201,000		Add ≈
koi garden		110,000		Add ≈
koi pond		90,500		Add ≈
pond koi		90,500		Add ≈
fish koi		74,000		Add ≈
koi fish		74,000		Add ≈
koi tattoo		49,500		Add ≈
japanese koi		33,100		Add ≈
koi sale		27,100		Add ≈
koi for sale		22,200		Add ≈
koi tattoos		22,200		Add ≈
japanese koi carp		14,800		Add ≈
koi ponds		14,800		Add ≈
ponds koi		14,800		Add ≈
koi food		12,100		Add ≈
koi koi		9,900		Add ≈
koi supplies		8,100		Add ≈
koi water		8,100		Add ≈
koi pond pump		4,400		Add ≈
koi uk		4,400		Add ≈
koi carp pond		3,600		Add ≈
koi carp ponds		3,600		Add ≈
koi pictures		3,600		Add ≈
black koi		2,900		Add ≈
japanese koi fish		2,900		Add ≈
koi art		2,900		Add ≈
koi forum		2,900		Add ≈
richdon koi		2,400		Add ≈
butterfly koi		1,900		Add ≈
large koi		1,900		Add ≈
koi drawing		1,600		Add ≈

there is a much longer tail of search queries related to koi than for goldfish.

Again, Bob downloads the results – broad and exact matches – into Excel, for future reference.

Bob is a pretty conscientious guy, so he diligently inputs his whole list of terms into the Google Keyword Tool, five or so at a time, looking for patterns and volumes of demand. He also downloads them all for later. Here are some of his notes:

- 'gold fish' as two words gets an estimated search volume of 49,500 searches per month – more than for 'japanese koi' and 'koi carp fish' combined!
- 'pet fish' gets an estimated average search volume of

over 800,000 a month. Name the new website 'Bob's Pet Fish'?

- 'tropical fish' and 'aquarium fish' get volumes in the hundreds of thousands. 'Bob's Tropical Fish Emporium'? But goldfish aren't tropical!
- Around 9,900 people out there type the exact phrase 'goldfish bowl' into Google each month, and 2,400 type 'goldfish bowls'. 'Glass', 'plastic', 'round', 'small', 'cheap', 'traditional', 'accessories' and 'UK' are qualifiers.
- Searches for 'oranda', 'ranchu' and 'shubunkin' appear to be growing. Check again in two months?

Based on his research into what people are asking Google for, Bob eventually decides to do the following:

- Set up a new trading name of Bobs Pet Fish.
- Name the site www.BobsPetFish.co.uk.
- Eventually expand the range into aquarium and tropical fish, using the following sections on the new website: Bob is also using 'pet fish', 'tropical fish' and 'aquarium fish'.
- Include a 'goldfish bowls' section, discussing the pros and cons (some are just too small for happy fish) and offering large (5 gallon) bowls, with a filter included.
- Write a detailed content plan based on the demand research.
- Change his name by deed poll to Bob Spetfish[1].

3.4 EXPANDING YOUR VOCABULARY

In addition to the methods employed by Bob in the previous section, there are a few more ways of gaining inspiration for searches.

---

[1] Bob's a thorough kind of guy.

1. A good thesaurus is an excellent place to start, but think of not only the words in which you are interested, but also the words that a person might use with them (listing, buy, cheap, clearance, find, best, review).

2. Wordnet is a collection of words and the relationships between words – a kind of souped-up thesaurus. The software itself is available on the web at http://wordnetweb.princeton.edu/perl/webwn. It's not the friendliest user interface in the world, but it's worth persevering with for general subject areas, at least. Enter a word you want to investigate (start with simple nouns and verbs). Click the blue-underlined S to show the 'synset' – the set of related words, and:

   - click 'full hyponym' to see more specific concepts;
   - click 'inherited hypernym' to see less specific concepts;
   - click 'derivationally related form' to see words from similar roots;
   - click 'part meronym' to see a list of parts of the concept.

   Some attempts have been made to give WordNet a simpler interface. See http://kylescholz.com/projects/wordnet/ and http://www.visualthesaurus.com/ (this one charges for the service).

3. Try Google Sets http://labs.google.com/sets as mentioned in section 2.5.

4. Consider questions about your subject. Try adding 'how', 'what', 'who', 'when', 'where', 'why' or 'which' to words describing your topic of interest, and then running some Google keyword searches on them to gain some insight into question formats.

5. Google some of the words and look for other related words in the titles of the results.

3.5 WRITING FOR YOUR USERS

Hopefully, you now have some idea of what people want, and how they express those desires to Google. You are now in a position to respond to those desires, by writing about them, reflecting the vocabulary used by the people doing the searching.

Three things to do before beginning to write:

- Have a picture of who you're writing for in front of you as you write. Use made-up characters to represent the different types of user (in the writing trade these are known as **personas**). Make sure they each have a photo. Write a little bit about each of them – what they want, why they want it, and how they speak about it. Continually refer to them as you write.
- Define **overall aims**. These usually include answering the following questions: What am I offering? What problem does my idea or offering solve? Why is it worth trying and buying? Who is my target audience? Who am I and what are my credentials? Who are my competitors and how am I different from them? What resistance or objections will people have to this? What is the purpose of my pitch? When, where and how do I want people to take action?
- Define **aims for each piece of copy**. For each piece you should define: the customer need you are filling; identified words and phrases to include; the specific customer action to encourage. Don't bog down copy with a long list of keywords. If it doesn't fit, re-assign the phrase to another piece of copy.

Five things to keep in mind as you go along:

- **Chop.** Page content that is unrelated to the featured item or subject should be reduced to a minimum.

Write long and cut short – once you have written a piece, go back through it and cut it by a third of its length. Strive for precision and concision. Do this by:

- removing subjective adjectives (and most superlatives) such as 'superb' or 'amazing'. They are fine for ad copy, but for serious, honest discussion of a subject, their use should be infrequent;
- replacing passive sentences with active ones. Instead of 'a study was made of bananas' try 'we made a study of bananas';
- using bulleted lists (just like this one), but make sure they are more than a list of phrases – whole sentences are best;
- removing unnecessary definitions and explanations.

- **Chunk.** Chunk text into self-sufficient, headed, digestible paragraphs. Use headings, subheadings and sub-subheadings (and further, if necessary, up to six levels of subheading in extreme cases). Headings and subheadings should be clearly related to the subsequent content, so don't be afraid to repeat important words from the heading in the paragraph(s) that follow.
- **Check.** Check grammar, check spelling and check facts. Always have at least one other person proofread your writing. Always!
- **Strengthen.** Thematic words contained within a heading should be repeated in the succeeding paragraph(s). Don't be afraid to re-use the same words, but don't get carried away; the text must read as normal English. Make use of emboldening to highlight important words and phrases within the body of the text. This can also help the online reader to scan the page more efficiently.

- **Focus.** Each page should have a single top-level heading describing the entire subject focus of the page. Anything that a user might search for – be it a concept, a product, information or a feature – should eventually have a single page devoted to it and it alone, if the user is prepared to dig deep enough or refine their search enough. Synonyms, abbreviations (if any) and related phrases should all appear within the body of the text. Remember that any page may become the first page someone sees of your site.

The Most Important Thing: Be Useful

Your site has to be worth reading. This means writing good, useful content, which is not easy. The rest of the world writes to pander to the mass media[1]. This is not what you are going to do. You are going to write for your users, not for journalists (keep that for the press releases). Write great things for your users and you'll get links, in time. Not just any links. Authoritative, relevant sites will start to link to yours.

3.6 CREATING COPY

Different kinds of copy need different emphases.

- **Sales copy** – avoid a barrage of positive adjectives. Don't just list features, state benefits. Avoid clichés[2].
- **Informational copy** – found in your FAQ and customer support pages. Edit hard for concision. No flowery language.
- **Notification copy** – dead or mistyped links, credit-card acceptance confirmations, mistakes during

---

[1] See www.fark.com/2007/book/chapter1.shtml. The fools!
[2] Avoid them like the plague.

form-filling. All these events require notification, either positive or negative. Make it clear and concise, explaining what may have gone wrong and how to put it right.

The design of content pages varies, but there are some classic conventions for an article page in particular that are worth following:

- **The main headline**. This should label the article accurately and succinctly.
- **The lead-in.** Shocking, informative, fascinating, or sexy. Often a single sentence or set of fragments. Often differentiated through typographic styling from the rest of the article.
- **The first proper paragraph**. Following on from the catchy, flashy lead-in, the next task is to sum up the themes of what is to follow on the page. This will often include a first reference to the main call-to-action of the article, placed here so that impatient readers can get straight to their goal ('Yes, I like it, where do I buy it?') without having to read more than the article summary. More patient types should get a repeat of this call-to-action at the end of the article.
- **Other paragraphs**. Front-loaded with the important theme of the paragraph, and then expanding on it.
- **Subheadings.** When people read a web page, they tend to scan, rather than reading every word. Intersperse your paragraphs with appropriate sub-headings.
- **The last paragraph.** Leaves 'em wanting more (preferably with a smile). It should also include (or be followed by) a final call-to-action for the user – make it clear what they should do next!

This is by no means the only way to write an article, but it is a robust and proven structure for informational writing.

3.7 CONSTRUCTING A DETAILED CONTENT BRIEF

Now that you have explored what your users want, and learned more about how to create content for them, it is time to construct a detailed content brief. However, before getting stuck into this, you might like to dip into section 3.8 Advanced Search Demand Analysis, where we describe a depth of research into your users' goals and needs that can help you take the Relevance of your site to a whole new level. It is fairly advanced and can be skipped over if you have a relatively small site, but as your content grows and the range of goals that your customers express in search expands, the deeper your analysis of the long tail, the greater the benefit to your site's overall Relevance. It's tough going in places, but then nothing worth having is ever easy!

For now, let's assume you have enough knowledge of what your users want and let's plan a website for them.

A content brief is a page-by-page plan of what you are going to write for your site. The content brief will need to consider not just attracting people to click through from Google, but also the overall site strategy:

- who the site audience might be and what goals they might have (sometimes described through a set of visitor archetypes called personas, which we mentioned in section 3.5);
- how best to support their goals, and how and when to persuade them to take actions that you want them to take (sometimes called a persuasion architecture or persuasion paths);
- how to divide up and label the site's material (sometimes called its information architecture).

The strategy will be informed by the results of your user demand analysis, often (and preferably) supplemented by, but not dependent on, user interviews, focus groups, surveys and other market research; yes, your website is your organisation in microcosm.

If you have an existing site, a round of user research on your own and competitor sites can bring to the surface a number of goals that may not be apparent without observing user behaviour – determining what they do, rather than just what they say.

User goals that may not be found in the user demand analysis include 'unvoiced' goals and goals that are triggered by material on the site. Examples include personal relevance concerns (Is this aimed at me?); safety concerns (Who are these guys? Are they trustworthy?); telephoning (I don't want to sound stupid on the phone); relationship quality (I want to feel cared about); comparison (I want to compare their services with others); costs (How much is it? In total?); recommendations (Who else uses this?); sales concerns (Are the salespeople pushy?) to name but a few.

Information from site analytics[1] about recorded behaviours may also be included, as well as business analyses of competitor strengths and weaknesses.

If you have an existing site, you may also wish to take an inventory of existing content, and how it might be reworked according to the new site strategy.

3.7.1 Laying Out a Content Brief

We recommend that each page in the content brief should define the following elements:

---

[1] See chapter 6 Using Google to Grow: Better Lovin'.

Title	The page title that will appear in Google's search results.
Description	The page description that will appear in Google's search results.
Headings	Each of the main headings on the page. This may be just the first heading, or it may be all headings, depending on the complexity of the page.
Purpose	What is the purpose of the page? For example, an article page might need to:

An article page might need to:

- satisfy a visitor's requirement for information;
- point them towards information about products that might solve their problem;
- encourage in-linking and sharing.

An article navigation page might need to:

- clearly lay out a set of themes to be explored;
- promote new and popular articles.

Key vocabulary	Vocabulary derived from the user demand analysis that should be included on this page.
Key action	After reading the page, what next? Detail the action that you hope the visitor will take. This may be 'progress deeper into site', 'click more information button' or 'submit form'. If the visitor does not take this action, the page can be considered to have failed in its purpose.

Links to other pages   Anchor text[1] and targets of the import-
                                    ant links on the page to other pages on
                                    the site (standard menu links that appear
                                    on every page may be assumed and
                                    ignored). For example: About Us
                                    [/about-us.html]

Links to other sites   Anchor text and targets of links to other
                                    sites. For example: World Wide Web
                                    Consortium [http://www.w3.org]

Example

Title   Goldfish Disease, Symptoms and Causes –
                      Bobspetfish.co.uk

Description   A detailed look at diseases of goldfish, the
                      symptoms to look out for, and the common
                      causes behind them.

Headings   H1: Goldfish Diseases
                              H2: Common Goldfish Disease Symptoms
                                H3: Dropsy or bloating
                                H3: Swim bladder problems
                                H3: Eye problems
                                  H4: Cloudy eye
                                H3: Mouth problems
                                H4: Mouth rot
                                H3: Gill problems
                                H3: Scale and skin problems
                                  H4: Lumps, ulcers and cysts
                                H3: Fin problems

---

[1] Anchor text was discussed in section 2.6 Assessing the Authority of Content.

H4: Fin rot
H4: Tail rot
H2: Parasites of Goldfish
H3: Ich or ick (ichthyophthiriasis)
H3: Velvet, rust and gold spot (oodinium)
H3: Worms (fluke)
H3: Anchorworm
H3: Fish lice
H3: White spot disease
H3: Neon tetra disease
H2: Infectious Diseases in Goldfish
H3: Bacterial infections
H3: Fungus and fungal infection
H3: Viral infections
H4: Lymphocystis

Purpose	Satisfy visitor's need to diagnose problem If not, guide to email contact form Suggest treatments where possible Encourage in-linking and sharing
Key vocabulary	disease, diseases, illness, illnesses, health, problems, sick, pond, tank, aquarium
Key action	Continue to treatment article OR email contact form
Links to other pages	[treatment name] treatment article [aquarium water quality] water quality article [genetic problems] goldfish breeding article [injuries] treating goldfish injuries article
Links to other sites	http://en.wikipedia.org/wiki/List_of_aquarium_diseases

Pages can be grouped by type. Usability research[1] has suggested a division of site content into three types of page:

1. **Transaction Pages** (sometimes called 'action pages'). These require input from the visitor in some way, such as entering credit card details or a mailing address.
2. **Informational Pages** (sometimes called 'content pages'). These provide information to satisfy a goal held by the visitor. A classic example would be a product information page in a catalogue site, or a description of an individual service, or an article about a particular subject. This is where the bulk of the content is kept.
3. **Navigation Pages** (sometimes called 'category pages'). These direct a visitor through the site. Navigation pages can be subdivided into further types:
   • **Home Page**. The very first navigation page many visitors encounter, which needs to indicate the goals that can be accomplished on the entire site, and establish a sense of trust and belonging. It is a starting point for many journeys, but don't forget that it is not the only starting point; users coming from Google may arrive on your site at any page.
   • **Main Navigation Pages**. Drawn from the information architecture, the primary way of chunking and labelling the content of the site, usually linked to from the main navigation bar on each page. The content should be succinct[2] while making clear what the navigation choices are. A classic example would be a category page in

---

[1] Source: Web Usability Partnership Ltd
[2] A common usability issue on websites is placing extensive content on a navigation page, which can result in the user being distracted from their goal, or being confused as to how to proceed.

a catalogue site, but any page between the home page and the final user goal can be thought of as a navigation page.

- **Theme Navigation Pages** (sometimes called 'cross-cutting navigation pages' or 'demand pages'). Pages constructed to respond to types of user demand not catered for in the main navigation pages. For example, if your site is a clothing retail site and the main navigation pages chunk up content firstly by purpose of clothing, then by type of clothing, then by fit, theme navigation pages may separately chunk all the content into primary categories such as ladies' clothing, cheap clothing, red clothing. Any single informational page may be linked to from several different theme pages, as in the case of a ladies' cheap red jacket. By choosing a main navigation structure, you are not prevented from creating additional navigation themes. Theme navigation pages are typically linked to from right-hand boxes, or page footers, or even just through a site map. Remember that a theme navigation page will often be the first page a visitor sees when arriving from Google, so it needs to provide some home page functions as well.

By the end of the detailed content brief, you should be well on the way to producing the content for your website. Cross-reference from your list of user goals and your list of vocabulary from your user demand analysis, and ensure that you have not missed any.

A couple of tips and tricks to finish:

- **The jargon-buster**. Write out a lengthy glossary of terms specific to your niche (look ahead to Lists in section 5.1.2 Telling Google about Blocks of Text for details of how to present these in HTML and make good use of it). Where a term deserves a lengthy explanation, give one in a separate short article.

- **Tagging.** Many content management systems provide a fast way to generate theme navigation pages through the use of 'tags'. An author can 'tag' their document with a number of words describing its content. The user sees these usually as a list at the foot (sometimes the head) of the page; clicking on one brings up a list of all pages tagged with that word.

Finally, its time to start writing (or hand the brief to a good copywriter) – good luck! For further ideas about content, rather than the specifics of its creation, look ahead to chapter 4 Enhance Your Site's Reputation, where you will learn to take your website into a different league.

3.8 ADVANCED SEARCH DEMAND ANALYSIS

For many smaller websites, the Google Keyword Tool discussed in section 3.3 is powerful, free and, crucially, sufficient to get enough insight into the needs and goals of users. It does have its limits, however, and is typically inadequate for all but the simplest analysis that a bigger website may need. If you have a smaller website and a limited budget, then this Advanced Search Demand Analysis section may be of theoretical interest only. It isn't required reading, as the use of these advanced techniques requires access to search data that is typically too expensive for smaller sites. This section does, however, provide an insight into the power of detailed search demand analysis and the opportunities it provides to website owners trying to maximise the traffic they acquire from natural search. So you can either read on to see what may be down the road for you, or skip forward to the next chapter.

The Google Keyword Tool tells you about the most important searches it sees, but it does not return all of the patterns within the long tail for a particular query. Consider a slow day for Google, in which only five queries were made:

- Why do fools fall in love?
- Why do birds sing?
- Why do birds sing so gay?
- Why do they fall in love?
- Why do birds suddenly appear every time you are near?

If this were actually true, you could tell from the Google Keyword Tool that 'Why do birds sing' was searched for twice (once on its own, once as part of 'Why do birds sing so gay?'). It is more interesting that 'Why do birds' appears in 60% of all searches and that 'Why do' appears in 100% of all searches, but the Google Keyword Tool does not appear to return these kinds of patterns, even though they can be extremely important insights into how to construct pages so that they align themselves with the way people search.

Example

In the travel sector, many searches are highly specific and geographic in nature. Few people type in 'hotels' – they want 'boutique hotels in Somerset', 'tourist hotels in Kuala Lumpur', and indeed 'tourist hotels in Koala Lumper'. As the searches tend to be first narrowed down by place and only then narrowed down by style or facility, it would be easy to miss the 'tourist hotels' and 'boutique hotels' searches if you were looking only at the head of this long tail.

The Google Keyword Tool is also limited in the number of results it returns. To get further under the skin of all those searches, you need to build a more substantial set of data about words and phrases in searches that deliver visitors to websites in your sector; a list of queries at least tens, if not hundreds, of thousands long.

Such lists include the long tail of queries that individually may be responsible for a mere handful of visitors. Even so, the long tail in total is responsible for more overall traffic than the more popular queries at the head[1].

Example

In a real set of search queries delivering visitors to the consumer electronics sector, the most popular query was typed in 13,070 times. The thousandth most popular query delivered just 149 visitors.

The number of visitors delivered by the top thousand queries was one third of the total – two thirds of the visitors were delivered by the rest.

Happily, there are bigger and better sources of data out there than those Google makes available. These allow you to start investigating the long tail of search queries typed into Google.

Case Study

Channel 4 called us in to analyse the search demand around homes and DIY. We built a list of over 10,000 unique home and DIY-related search queries that

---

1 Revisit section 1.2 Organising the World's Information for further details on the long tail.

delivered over 2,000,000 visitors between them to various sites. After a detailed analysis we uncovered a number of interesting patterns of vocabulary to target. Among several other insights, we found a lot of demand for 'how to' do things related to home improvement and DIY, such as how to fit a laminate floor, or how to convert a loft – the wide variety of objects of the 'how to' searches meant that collectively they became significant, but individually, when considering the 'what' they were trying to find out 'how to' do, they would not have been spotted without investigating the long tail.

Channel 4 duly made changes to information pages that they had already produced on the objectives of the 'how to' but now referred to them with 'how to' in all the important places in the structure of the pages. They saw an increase in traffic to this information of 370% as a result.

3.8.1 Getting Large Data Sets

Some sources of large sets of data include:

- Experian Hitwise (data provenance: licensed from ISPs, UK focused)
- Word Tracker (data provenance: licensed from Dogpile search engine, US focused)
- Keyword Discovery (data provenance: user panel through toolbar, US focused)
- Wordze (data provenance: licensed from ISPs and toolbar panel, US focused)

For the UK market, Experian Hitwise is hard to beat, and was used in the Channel 4 case study – although it doesn't come cheap. Hitwise provides aggregated data collected from a number of ISP[1] companies in the UK. This means Hitwise has a record of everything the customers of those companies do online (anonymised, of course): the websites they visit, the search engines they use, what they type into search engines and which search results they then click on. Hitwise states that the data relates to the internet usage of more than 8 million UK internet users.

The Hitwise data allows you to see exactly which search engine queries are delivering traffic to which websites. The list of websites must be defined by you – either by listing competitor sites, or by using the Hitwise 'search term analysis' tool, where you type in a search term and are returned a list of sites that win significant volumes of traffic from that term. Once you have your 'custom category', you can then download a fairly large number of unique search expressions that delivered data – around 50,000 unique search expressions over any 12-week period. You can download several 12-week sets and amalgamate them – we typically download the last four quarters of data to cover seasonality, then merge them and remove any duplicates.

This ability to investigate only those queries that are already delivering visitors to sites of interest is of great value to sites trying to be more relevant to the market represented by those visitors.

3.8.2 Analysing a Large Data Set

Remember all those lists of key phrases and volumes that Bob downloaded? Well, go and do the same for your site, take all of the exact match lists, and put them all together in one large CSV[2] file. Alternatively, if you can afford it, and especially if your sector is highly competitive, go and get your several-thousand-row Hitwise download.

---

[1] Internet Service Providers – the people who provide your internet access.

[2] It stands for comma separated value. No formatting or functions. Just values.

Cleaning the Data

First, remove the columns that aren't required. The only ones you are really interested in for this exercise are the 'Keywords' column and the 'Search Volume' column in the case of Google Keyword Tool data (the 'percentage of total visitors' in Hitwise).

The next challenge is to remove the duplicates, to avoid double counting. You did download the exact matches, didn't you?[1] You did? Excellent. Now you are likely to have a number of repeated rows, so you need to remove those. You can do this by hand for a small list, but for a file several thousand rows long some programmatic help will be needed.

There are a number of programs that can help – CSV Easy[2] is rather good, but you can also perform analyses using a number of database or spreadsheet programs, albeit less elegantly. If you are using CSV Easy, just open the file, click the 'deduplication' button on the toolbar, and select the column to deduplicate – 'keywords' in the case of Google Keyword Tool data. Easy as that. Don't forget to save the result.

Panning for Gold

Your next task is to search for patterns. This involves looking for all occurrences of a word (or part of a word) throughout the data, and summing the results. Let's look at two ways of doing this.

1. **CSV Easy**. Open the CSV and click the filter button (the one with the funnel on it) on the toolbar. In the Filter dialogue box, click 'Add' to add a new rule, select 'Keywords' as the column, and 'contains' as the condition. In the value field, enter the word (or part of word) you are interested in. For example, if you were researching women's clothing, you might enter 'women' so that you

---

[1] You didn't? Go and get them. We'll wait.
[2] http://www.tizma.com/csveasy/

pick up 'women', 'women's' and the common misspelling 'womens'. If you wanted to pick up 'woman' as well, you could select 'regular expression' as the condition, and enter '.*wom.n.*' as the value (regular expressions are very useful for searching for patterns, but somewhat outside the scope of this book; you can learn more about them at http://en.wikipedia.org/wiki/Regular_expression). Click 'data analysis' in the menu bar to sum the result.

CSV Easy have also (kindly and at our request) included a rather nifty text-mining function. This allows you to run a phrase occurrence analysis, returning a list of one, two, three and four-word phrases in order of frequency of occurrence in the data. It also allows you to specify lists of synonyms for the mining; for example, you may be interested in patterns of demand for women's clothing, so provide a synonyms list of 'women's, womens, ladies, lady's, girls, female'. In the results, all these words would be considered variations of 'women's' and their occurrences counted accordingly. Careful use of this alongside the filter function results in a powerful way of analysing the long tail.

2. **Excel**. Open the CSV and save it as an Excel file. Add a row above it all. Put your chosen word (or part of word) in a cell to the right of 'Search Volume' (cell C2, if you only have the 'Keywords' and 'Search Volume' columns). Now here comes the formula: in cell C3, enter =IF((ISNUMBER(FIND(C$2,$A3)))=TRUE,$B3,0)

Broken down, this says that if a search for the string 'care' within the string 'goldfish care' returns an error, then the value is 0. If the search returns a result (any result), then the value is whatever is in B3 – in this case 22,200. This formula can then be copied down the column. To sum the entire column, enter =SUM(C3:C152) (assuming you only have 152 lines of data) in cell C1.

Copy column C across so that you have several columns, each summed at the top, so that you can compare several words at once.

goldfish keyword volumes.xlsx - Microsoft Excel

K1 =SUM(K3:K152)

	A	B	C	D	E	F	G	H	I	J	K	L
1		Column Total:	34,570	30,140	23,800	28,970	16,167	22,570	15,560	17,859	18,700	12,988
2	Keyword	Search volume	bowl	care	aquarium	tank	fancy	pond	memory	breed	disease	fantail
3	goldfish	1,220,000	0	0	0	0	0	0	0	0	0	0
4	goldfish bowl	33,100	33,100	0	0	0	0	0	0	0	0	0
5	goldfish care	22,200	0	22,200	0	0	0	0	0	0	0	0
6	goldfish aquarium	22,200	0	0	22,200	0	0	0	0	0	0	0
7	goldfish tank	18,100	0	0	0	18,100	0	0	0	0	0	0
8	fancy goldfish	14,800	0	0	0	0	14,800	0	0	0	0	0
9	pond goldfish	14,800	0	0	0	0	0	14,800	0	0	0	0
10	goldfish memory	14,800	0	0	0	0	0	0	14,800	0	0	0
11	goldfish fish	14,800	0	0	0	0	0	0	0	0	0	0
12	goldfish breeding	12,100	0	0	0	0	0	0	0	12,100	0	0
13	goldfish diseases	12,100	0	0	0	0	0	0	0	0	12,100	0
14	fantail goldfish	12,100	0	0	0	0	0	0	0	0	0	12,100
15	goldfish food	12,100	0	0	0	0	0	0	0	0	0	0
16	goldfish water	5,900	0	0	0	0	0	0	0	0	0	0
17	pet goldfish	5,900	0	0	0	0	0	0	0	0	0	0
18	goldfish types	5,900	0	0	0	0	0	0	0	0	0	0
19	goldfish pictures	5,900	0	0	0	0	0	0	0	0	0	0
20	comet goldfish	8,100	0	0	0	0	0	0	0	0	0	0
21	oranda goldfish	8,100	0	0	0	0	0	0	0	0	0	0
22	goldfish for sale	8,100	0	0	0	0	0	0	0	0	0	0
23	goldfish live	8,100	0	0	0	0	0	0	0	0	0	0
24	goldfish disease	6,600	0	0	0	0	0	0	0	0	6,600	0
25	red goldfish	6,600	0	0	0	0	0	0	0	0	0	0

Sheet1 Sheet2 Sheet3

Ready | Average: 248 | Count: 152 | Sum: 37,400 | 100%

This example has 152 rows of data – the top 25 are shown. You can immediately see that although 'goldfish diseases' is searched for 12,100 times compared to 14,800 each for 'fancy goldfish', 'pond goldfish' and 'goldfish memory', the word 'disease' is actually responsible for 18,700 searches across the data set (it appears in both 'goldfish disease' and 'goldfish diseases'). This makes 'disease' a more important term than 'fancy', 'pond', 'memory' (or 'breed').

Example: Pattern-finding

A long tail of queries delivering visits to food-based websites was investigated using the text-mining tools in CSV Easy, searching for two, three and four-word patterns. The tool revealed the following generic (i.e. not brand-based) pattern as responsible for the greatest number of visits in the data analysed:

recipe for	3.79%

That's right, the two-word pattern 'recipe for' was responsible for 3.79% of all traffic into the food-related sites investigated. The pattern actually includes plurals ('recipes for') and common mis-spellings found in the data (receipe, recipies, recepies), thanks to some pre-processing of the data to define these as synonyms.

The most popular generic three or four-word queries were:

how to make	0.81%
how to cook	0.30%
Total	**1.11%**

Just these two phrases were responsible for over 1% of all visits into the sector. As a comparison, 'how do you make' was responsible for 0.07%, leaving 'how to make' a clear winner for 'how-to' articles.

The next few most popular three or four-word phrases were individual recipes. These would appear to be the things that the British public would like to make and don't already have a recipe for:

carrot cake recipe	0.20%
toad in the hole	0.18%
bread and butter pudding	0.16%
sweet and sour	0.16%
corned beef hash	0.14%
chocolate cake recipe	0.14%
fairy cake recipe	0.13%
yorkshire pudding recipe	0.13%
Total	**1.24%**

The phrases 'carrot cake recipe' and 'toad in the hole' may well have been returned by the Google Keyword Tool too, as they are likely to exist as stand-alone search phrases, as well as being parts of other, longer phrases (such as 'easy carrot cake recipe' or 'simple carrot cake recipe'). Note that Google, while fairly good at grouping similar words in search, does not display 'recipes' in the Keyword Tool analysis of 'recipe', so 'recipe' and 'recipes' are considered as separate words. 'Sweet and sour' probably would not have been returned as a term by the Google Keyword Tool, as although it is a part of many phrases, it would be very unlikely to exist as a stand-alone search phrase.

Some further investigation using the regular expression filter shows how many keywords follow the pattern '[something] recipe'[1]. The result? Over 20% of all searches matched this pattern.

Assuming that you want to construct a page around sweet and sour, what exactly should it cover? First you must investigate how 'sweet and sour' queries break down. You can do this simply by filtering the original data set for all occurrences of 'sweet and sour'.

sweet and sour chicken	0.03%
sweet and sour sauce	0.02%
sweet and sour sauce recipe	0.02%
sweet and sour pork	0.01%
sweet and sour chicken recipe	0.01%
sweet and sour pork recipe	0.01%
sweet and sour	0.01%
sweet and sour sauce recipes	0.01%
sweet and sour recipe	0.01%
ken hom sweet and sour sauce	0.01%
sweet and sour recipes	0.01%
recipe for sweet and sour fish	0.01%
easy sweet and sour chicken	0.01%
sweet and sour recipies	0.01%
recipe for sweet and sour chicken	0.01%
Total	**0.16%**

You should already begin to see how an article (or set of articles) might be constructed to meet these demands – but beware of being too specific.

Don't forget, it's the overall patterns that have the value, as they say something about how users express their goals and how a website needs to be constructed to be relevant to them.

---

[1] As a regular expression this would be written .*(recipe|recipes)$ – the . means 'any character', the * means 'any number of times', the | means 'or' and the $ means 'this is the end of the phrase'.

3.8.3 Creating a Taxonomy of Demand

You have by now obtained a set of phrases which represent patterns of demand to target. The list must next be organised into groups based on the family relationships between them – a taxonomy. Google groups sets of concepts together, so you should too, as best you can.

Taxonomies can be automatically generated from large datasets – there are a number of algorithms out there that work on concepts such as co-occurrence of phrases in documents, but the average human is quite good at this sort of task without automated help. This is commonly approached as a simple 'card-sorting' exercise, where all of the expressed demand patterns identified can be written onto cards (or scraps of paper) and then sorted into piles. Or you can just put them into a spreadsheet.

This taxonomy may well reflect the eventual structure of your website – even if not, it will certainly inform it. The taxonomy should arrange demand in terms of specificity, starting at the bottom with the most specific concepts and grouping them into more general ones labelled by less specific terms, and so on up the chain. If you find yourself tempted to make up a label, check it first against your dataset – there may be a better alternative.

Finally, don't forget that there are likely to be several different valid taxonomies – many different categories can all lead to the same final destinations. Such cross-cutting categories can be supported by the themed navigation discussed in section 3.7.1 Laying out a Content Brief.

Example: Creating taxonomies

Taking the sweet and sour example above, certain family relationships can be seen. The concept of 'sweet and sour pork recipe' is pretty much the same as 'how to make sweet and sour pork', so these should be gathered together within a single page. This might be as a heading and subheading.

Recipes
   Sweet and sour recipes
      Sweet and sour sauce
         Sweet and sour pork recipe | How to make sweet and sour pork
         Sweet and sour chicken recipe | How to make sweet and sour chicken
         Sweet and sour fish recipe | How to make sweet and sour fish

Don't forget that there is more than one way of grouping:

Alternative 1
Recipes
   Pork recipes
      Sweet and sour pork | How to make sweet and sour pork
   Chicken recipes
      Sweet and sour chicken recipe | How to make sweet and sour chicken
   Fish recipes
      Sweet and sour fish | How to make sweet and sour fish
   Sauce recipes
      Sweet and sour sauce recipe | How to make sweet and sour sauce

Alternative 2
Recipes
  Sauce recipes
    Chinese recipes
      Sweet and sour sauce recipe | How to make sweet and sour sauce
      Recipes using sweet and sour sauce
      Sweet and sour pork | How to make sweet and sour pork
      Sweet and sour chicken recipe | How to make sweet and sour chicken
      Sweet and sour fish | How to make sweet and sour fish

Alternative 3
Recipes
  Chinese recipes
    Chinese chicken recipes
      Sweet and sour chicken recipe | How to make sweet and sour chicken

3.8.4 Concluding Your Advanced Search Demand Analysis

If you are here, we've managed to drag you through some of the more intense guidance of the book, so well done. Let's just recap the purpose of such advanced analysis:

- The long tail of search goals expressed by users is full of information about how to build a profoundly relevant site for your market; it's just hard and expensive to get out the insights.
- Analysing large sets of data is complex and requires new

skills or new activities to secure the benefits that are always[1] available in the data.

- Creating detailed structured taxonomies of demand means comprehensive coverage of the ways that your users express their needs and high levels of natural search traffic to boot.

50 WAYS . . .

2. Admit you don't really know what your users want and commit yourself to finding out by doing research into how they express themselves to Google. *See section 3.1*

3. Think deep, think laterally and take your time when investigating the ways users search for the stuff on your website. *See section 3.2*

4. Get closer to what Google knows about the words in your marketplace. It knows a lot and will give it up if you ask it the right questions. *See section 3.4*

5. Chunk and repeat when writing for users and Google. *See section 3.5*

6. Create the quality content that your users want and need to find. This works for Google too. *See section 3.6.*

7. Always remember that the long tail exists – even if you can't see it – so err on the side of more content. *See section 3.7*

8. Be prepared to travel far down the long tail of search because there are always profitable surprises in the patterns and themes you'll find there. *See section 3.8*

9. Find the money to buy good quality search term data. It will be worth it. *See section 3.8.1*

10. Build your website's information architecture from a detailed taxonomy of demand. *See section 3.8.3*

---

[1] Okay, so not always. We have once failed to find insight in long tail data for a client, but only once, and that was because he had invented something that no-one was looking for. If there is no related demand for your product or service, then building a relevant site is a tough nut to crack.

4

ENHANCE YOUR SITE'S REPUTATION

Building Relevance to your users' goals into your site is how you assemble the first leg of the Tripod of Love, and as Relevance is everything to Google, your total commitment to its presence on your site is a necessity, not an option. Google needs Relevance as a foundation on which to grow its love for your site. Every effort you make in the service of your site's Relevance to your users' goals will repay you over and over. So, assuming you've got the message about Relevance, it's time to introduce Reputation, the next leg of the Tripod of Love. In a competitive market, Reputation rocks! It is what distinguishes one relevant site from another, and is the determining factor in Google's preference when faced with countless pages of otherwise relevant content.

If you avoided the detail in section 2.6 Assessing the Authority of Content, then we recommend that you pop back and read it now before moving on.

4.1 THE PRINCIPLES OF REPUTATION

Before we look at ways to make your website irresistible to the links you will need to compete for, there are three principles of Reputation that you must fully comprehend and embrace. They are:

1. Authority only links to value.
2. Word-of-mouth drives linking.
3. Links are to URLs not pages.

4.1.1 Authority Only Links to Value

It is not safe to assume that your site is naturally worth linking to, just because you have something to do with it. However invested you are in your website, the rest of the world is going to look at it with a pretty cold eye. Given that your aim is to develop its Reputation by acquiring links from sites with their own Reputation (remember this means with their own authority and Relevance), you have to be able to answer the question 'Why would they bother?' before you can hope to make progress. It is humans who make decisions about whether a link happens or not, and on the assumption that these humans are incorruptible and interested in linking only to information that is likely to be of interest to *their* website visitors, they will use pretty refined human capabilities when considering your site for a link. The single most powerful filter you can apply to your judgement of whether your site is likely to be favourably considered is that of 'value'. Ask yourself these questions:

- Will your site really be of value to the visitors of the sites you hope will link to it?
- Will they really be glad they clicked through to your site having seen a link to it?

This value can take many possible forms: financial, entertainment, educational, environmental, etc., but value your site must have, for without it, the links will simply not happen.

What does value look like, you may ask? Well, it's simple. You have to aim to be the best at what you do online. Simply the best. While you may never actually achieve this aim, your pursuit of it will be the only reliable way of acquiring the linking votes that will enhance your site's Reputation. At this point it may be worth reflecting on a few things, such as:

- your site's objectives;
- your business model;
- your competitors;
- and, hey, how much you can really be bothered about your hobby.

This book cannot now divert itself into a general exercise in business differentiation, but the reality is that there is so much average noisy ordinariness on the web that unless you raise your site up out of it you will be forever disappointed in the quality of links you acquire. While we can't devote thousands of words to telling you how to pursue excellence for your business model, we can devote a few to the pursuit of excellence for your website, which is what the rest of this chapter is about.

It is at this point that we usually jump up and down in meetings with businesses who are trying to do SEO[1] better. We're jumping up and down because we are trying to ram home the simple fact that SEO has just stepped beyond the remit of the IT or marketing teams and into the executive, and nobody was expecting that. Acquiring a competitive share of the natural visits that Google refers to websites in any sector requires a pursuit of online excellence which is *always* more commercial and operational than is expected. IT and marketing can only hope to influence such a pursuit, never attain it on their own. So before you do anything else – if you are not already part of your executive – try and schedule a meeting where you can introduce the idea that 'SEO is going to involve a bit more than we anticipated'.

Website owners who are used to generating their business through conventional channels, where locality and specialism are often sufficient to be a favoured supplier, can find the transition to irrelevance in Google's results rather painful. It

---

[1] This is Search Engine Optimisation; we haven't mentioned it for a while, so we thought a reminder would be helpful.

does require a new type of work within these organisations – a real operational change – to adapt to Google's version of the high street, and those that are changing fastest are the ones finding Google's love more forthcoming.

4.1.2 Word-of-Mouth Drives Linking

Let's assume that you have a wonderful new website and that it is already irresistible to links. Now you have this fabulously relevant site just oozing linkability we can introduce another conventional marketing approach: websites that are worthy of fantastic Reputation do not need intimidating marketing budgets to actually acquire it. Google's love is not directly related to the money you spend in the marketplace developing awareness of your proposition and your brand, and while there is an indirect relationship that we'll come to, sites that are worthy of links acquire them primarily because the humans on the web have really neat ways of sharing how impressed they are with them.

We use a concept with which most traditional businesses are very familiar when we discuss how knowledge of your fantastic website passes from person to person using the internet, and that is word-of-mouth. Word-of-mouth has always played a powerful role in marketing, whether deliberately pursued by the marketer or not, and has been written about very articulately by the likes of Malcolm Gladwell[1]. Conventional word-of-mouth has limitations: one person typically speaks to one other person at a time, and that person must remember and act on what they've heard, passing it on to others of their acquaintance. Online word-of-mouth, however, is a different beast all together. It has two major advantages over real-world word-of-mouth and they are:

---

[1] Malcolm Gladwell, *The Tipping Point: How Little Things Can Make A Big Difference*, Little, Brown, 2000

1. Online word-of-mouth is broadcast, not singlecast.
2. Online word-of-mouth is permanent[1].

Online, if you say something once in an email, on a blog, on Facebook or on Twitter then many people can read it. This means that a visitor to your site has power – as a distributor of enthusiasm about it – with exponential potential if a proportion of those reading about it decide to share the enthusiasm with their network of contacts too. And this same enthusiasm, once posted online, has a habit of sticking around almost indefinitely to be found and visited time and again.

Online word-of-mouth is how most sites that acquire rapid growth in links achieve it. They don't necessarily go looking for this to happen – as you will learn to do – it just tends to happen because, for one reason or another, the site or some of the information on it is perceived to be of great value to enough people for it to enjoy this word-of-mouth effect. It's not the mentions on, for example, Facebook and Twitter that actually constitute the valuable links – more on that later too – it's the fact that a proportion of the word-of-mouth reaches people who are able to create links on websites that have good Reputation, which can in turn pass some of it on to the site in question. These are the links that matter.

Section 4.2.3 Getting the Word Out covers in more detail the use of word-of-mouth in its web incarnation, 'social media', to help get the irresistible nature of your site in front of as many linking site owners as possible.

4.1.3 Links Are to URLs Not Pages

The final Reputation principle you need to accept is related to the technical 'addressability' of your pages of Reputation-worthy

---

[1] Well, almost. Not all web pages last forever.

content. You will know from your own experience that when you make a search, Google often suggests very specific pieces of information at very specific locations on the web and not just the home page of the website concerned. It does this because of its assessment of the Relevance of the information at that specific web address and because of the combined Reputation of the piece of information within the site it belongs to. We are deliberately avoiding using the word 'page' to refer to where this piece of 'information' resides, because Google doesn't have a concept of a page, it only has a place where information is found when it goes looking for it, and this is a web address, or a URL[1]. It is the difference between telling a friend to look at the Goldfish Care page of Bob's website and emailing the URL www.bobspetfish.co.uk/goldfish/goldfish-care/[2] to them; they have the same experience of a page of information, but only one of these is Google-readable, and that is the URL. Google's automatic collection of information from websites is therefore a collection of information at specific URLs. It is also these URLs that people link to, because you can't link to Bob's Goldfish Care page without one. Google is therefore assessing the Reputation of the information it finds at specific URLs.

So far, so good, but why is this significant? The reason is that if the same piece of important information resides at more than one URL on the same site, then those critical voting links from other sites may end up pointing at different locations when they really should point at one. One URL for the same piece of information is desirable because you want your site's Reputation to pool at a single location, so that Google can prefer it whenever it considers the information relevant to a particular search, and if users can find these URLs in order to link to them, Google doubtless will too. If Google can find more than one URL on

---

[1] Revisit section 2.3 Finding Web Pages for more details on how Google finds the stuff it indexes.

[2] This isn't a real web address, so please don't try visiting it.

your site for the same piece of information and can also find links coming in from different sources to them separately, you have a problem. This problem causes the dilution of Reputation because Google has to assess the Reputation of these pieces of information separately despite their being the same. You can probably guess whether being 'diluted' is a good thing to happen to any part of your site's Reputation[1].

Very few websites come out of the box, or are built, in such a way as to guarantee that the unique pieces of important information on them reside at only one URL each. The corollary of this is the creation of a management task for supervising the use of URLs as the locations for information on your site, in order to ensure that the Reputation it acquires flows in the most effective manner possible. The task becomes particularly challenging when you redevelop your website and all the URLs of all your information change as a result. This issue is dealt with in more detail in section 5.2 Managing Reputation Flow.

4.1.4 The Courage to Pursue a Real Reputation

The next section of this chapter will start looking in detail at many of the individual things you need to consider when improving the Reputation of your website. Before we begin, we think it would be helpful to pause for breath and to give you a simple mantra on which to base this work. Putting technical matters to one side for a moment, the challenge for you is that of building a 'real' reputation. A real reputation, as opposed to an artificial box-ticking attempt to gain Google's love, is one that combines a pursuit of excellence with the embrace of word-of-mouth. One that sees you engage with your marketplace in an authentic and genuine manner. One that sees you work with integrity towards the best possible service you can provide. One

---

[1] It's not: diluted Reputation will reduce the likelihood of the information concerned being considered useful by Google and its ranking will suffer as a result.

that sees you build Relevance and irresistibility at every opportunity. One that does not shy away from difficult customers or situations, but is honest and forthcoming. Real reputations are for the courageous. Very few website owners are truly courageous, so your opportunity for differentiation begins here.

4.2 BUILDING A REAL REPUTATION

Google says time and again that you should build your website for users, not for Google[1], which we think is an astonishing statement, and a sign of people's absolute vulnerability to Google's power. The fact that website owners would consider producing a site that was organised around the way a single technical visitor experiences it – potentially at the cost of the experience of real users and customers – is remarkable. Yet that is the world of today: a world where one business dominates the mediation between supply and demand on the internet and where a failure to respond to how it mediates your supply could be commercially catastrophic.

Of course Google is right: build your site for the users/customers in your marketplace and it is much more likely to be effective than a site that is skewed in its focus towards the needs of a large software entity. This fact doesn't stop many website owners attempting to build their site for Google, on the assumption that it will be quicker and cheaper to try and cheat Google into thinking their site is more useful than it actually is, than to actually create a genuinely useful site that might make a difference in its market.

Our view is simple: to compete in most markets online you have to pursue excellence not subterfuge, because excellence is the only way your site will be resilient to the inevitable changes in Google's approach to distributing its love. As we said in section 4.1.1 Authority Only Links to Value, this book cannot

---

[1] http://www.google.co.uk/support/webmasters/bin/answer.py?hl=en&answer=35769

drift into a general exposition on business excellence, but what we can do is look at how excellence online is directly related to Google's assessments of your site's Relevance and authority.

It is our assertion that only sites that can demonstrate conspicuous value to the users – not the owners – of the sites they want links from will enjoy a growth in links from those sites, as it is hard to imagine why the owner of a reputable site might want to link to anything that didn't demonstrate such value. And so, you may think, evaluating the sort of sites you might want links from could be a good place to start in deciding what sort of value you should offer. Well it could, but not in this book.

Shifting your focus away from what you can do best (namely being true to your organisation, yourself, your brand, your expertise, your specialism, your products, your services or whatever it is that gets you out of bed in the morning), towards some sort of masquerade where you don the mask of a site you hope will be valued, is an exercise doomed to mediocrity at best.

Building a real reputation is an exercise in personal, professional and organisational excellence, where striving to be the best online for your users is the only way to succeed. Really. No magic bullets here; building your Tripod of Love means hard work and dedication to the pursuit of something that is *real*.

To illustrate the concept of pursuing a real reputation, we are going to report on a conversation we had with fictional Bob Spetfish. We'd love this to be a dialogue directly with you (dear reader), but obviously it can't be, so we hope you will draw inspiration from Bob's example.

The Entrepreneurial Goldfish Family

It turns out that Bob is the fourth generation of an entrepreneurial goldfish family which in the past has played a key role in importing techniques and expertise from China, where the fish originate. Bob's great-grandfather travelled extensively in China, learning all that he could, and organised the painstaking export and transportation of rarer varieties. Bob's grandfather in turn was the genius behind the promotion of goldfish as prizes at carnivals and fairs, which, for the best part of 50 years, secured their success as a business, because they managed to make themselves a monopoly provider to the family-run fair businesses. Sadly, Bob's father was a bit of a drinker and got complacent with the business; he wasn't watching while breeding methods were modernised and prices for goldfish plummeted[1]. The new prices were irresistible to the fairs and other retail outlets who had been buying from the Goldfish Emporium run by Bob's family and they deserted their old supplier. Bob came into the business as a teenager and managed to help his dad salvage their own retail shop and a small group of select customers, collectors of the rare varieties that are still hard to find elsewhere. Bob retired his dad from the business a few years back.

One of the fascinating things about Bob's business is that the meticulous processes his great-grandfather set up, recording the sales of each variety in great detail, survived as good habits of the business. Bob now has almost 100 years of records of the goldfish business, plus a neat stack of diaries of his great-grandfather's travels to China in the early decades of the 20th Century. Bob's grandfather continued his father's passion for documenting the activities of the business; in addition, as an early amateur photographer, he collected a remarkable set of pictures of fairs and carnivals in pre- and post-war Britain, all with goldfish in the foreground! He also completed a complete photographic record of every variety of goldfish that ever passed through the business, in colour. These transparencies are sitting in a box under Bob's bed, and Bob knows that there haven't been any new varieties since the war, so this should be a complete record of all the varieties of goldfish.

---

[1] We'll draw breath at this point and apologise to anyone who knows a bit about the goldfish business. We are completely making it up as we go along.

When talking to Bob it is clear he has an encyclopedic knowledge of goldfish – less so of koi carp, as we will witness in section 5.2.3 – and is a very enthusiastic communicator about them. Bob left school at 16 in the 1980s to help his dad with the business, so missed out on the computer revolution that would have been present in his education from that point on. Consequently he knows little about the web or how it works, but has realised lately that pretty much everything, including goldfish, are available for sale there. Sensing an opportunity to grow the business with a website, Bob is swotting[1] up on all things web, but needs some help.

Bob has a number of advantages in his pursuit of excellence as a goldfish organisation and they largely comprise three things:

- the history of the business;
- the retained knowledge that Bob takes for granted;
- Bob's enthusiasm, which is into its third decade.

We will now look at how these advantages can be employed in the creation of a website with irresistible value to anyone who expresses their interest in goldfish to Google. The best way to approach this task is to separate what goes onto the site – its content[2] – from how it is supported by Bob's enthusiasm – his behaviour.

4.2.1 Head-turning Strategic Content of Great Value

To develop a real reputation for your content, it has to be exquisitely good. Don't be afraid of the high standards those words demand; excellence demands very high standards, and

---

[1] British slang for working intensively. Swots were the kids at school who were all work and no play.

[2] Content is allegedly still king after all (http://en.wikipedia.org/wiki/Web_content# Content_is_king).

you need to be up for the fight. In Bob's case we have come up with four content ideas to put on his site – in addition to the content already there for the fish he has for sale and their care, including the content he decided to create following his user demand work – which are going to take a lot of effort to pull together. Before we describe these ideas, please note that at no point have we worried about whether anyone is looking for this content. The combination of Bob's knowledge of goldfish and our experience of what works in developing Reputation inspires us to flesh out these ideas and get them built regardless. That's right, despite all our efforts so far in convincing you to build a site that is relevant to your users' goals, we are now encouraging Bob to do something that has no specific contextual justification. All we can say at this point is, trust us. It should be obvious why this will still work, once you've heard about these ideas. Okay, so, what are they?

1. An archive of Bob's great-grandfather's travelogues from his journeys in China researching and exporting huge numbers and varieties of goldfish. These were all handwritten, so Bob is painstakingly transcribing them to make their content completely visible to Google. He is also scanning the pages of the diaries themselves because there are sketches and maps and Chinese characters all over them; they really are fascinating documents. Finally, Bob is carefully working out the itineraries of the journeys and plotting them on maps to accompany the other information in the archive.

2. A light-hearted photo essay of the fairs and carnivals of Britain in the years preceding and following the Second World War, from the viewpoint of the goldfish given away as prizes at these events, as they still are today. Bob invites visitors to the site to submit their own photos, emulating his grandfather's, to continue the story into the new millennium. The photographers of the top three favourite

submissions at the end of each year's carnival season will be eligible for a goldfish bowl and two fish of their choice.

3. A photo library of all the common, comet, shubunkin and fancy varieties of goldfish, from his grandfather's store of photographs. Bob has decided he can't afford to pay a bureau to scan all the transparencies for him so he buys a second-hand machine on eBay, which does an excellent job of producing web images that are really good, even when zoomed into, and also print well up to about A4 paper size. He scans all the pictures, spends a while cleaning up the digital files, and then sells the scanner on eBay for little less than he paid for it. He ends up with a library of almost 200 images. He then makes the brave decision to allow people completely free access to all of them, including the higher resolution images for printing, under the Creative Commons[1] scheme.

4. A history of goldfish-buying trends in the UK over the last 100 years. Using the company's detailed records of sales of different varieties, Bob asks a friend of his, who is good with spreadsheets, to help him build some charts and graphs from the data that show trends and patterns in the share of total sales made up by individual varieties. Bob knows there is less data for the last few decades than for the company's heyday, but he is confident that the proportions the varieties sell in will still be pretty representative of the trends elsewhere in the market, despite the dip in sales. We decide that the trends for each variety should be shown on the home page of that variety on the site, which we hope will encourage links specific to that variety to point directly at the variety page and not at a general page showing all the trends.

5. A blog of Bob's efforts to turn his website into a cathedral of goldfish content. Bob has decided that he is going to

---

[1] http://en.wikipedia.org/wiki/Creative_Commons

emulate his great-grandfather and write a journal of his online travels to turn his struggling goldfish enterprise into a world leader. He hopes that people will find it personable and interesting, and that it will warm them to his business.

Joe Blogs

There's a great big blogosphere out there, full of people who all care enough about subjects to write about them. Sites such as technorati.com, bloglines.com and Google Blog Search allow you to search for bloggers who write about topics in which you have expertise. Ideally, find subject obsessives, not marketing people unless the latter are also genuinely passionate about their subject. If anything interesting comes up, write about it on your own site. Then let the blogger know that you have written about their post using a 'trackback' or 'ping-back', or even just a polite email. This is about building real relationships – friendships even – around a shared interest. Once again, be useful, polite and build on what others begin.

If you are having trouble finding inspiration, then go to http://www.google.co.uk/alerts/ and sign up for a news alert once a week, relating to your subject area. If too many stories are returned to deal with, find a more specific search phrase. Blog about any stories of interest. If you are of an academic bent, try http://scholar.google.co.uk/ to find academic papers which may be of interest to your audience and therefore worth commenting on.

Implementing all these content ideas is going to take a while, as there is a fair amount of labour involved in all of them, but Bob is relishing it; they are truly going to be a labour of love.

When we stop to look at the ideas we have conceived for Bob's website, we realise we have an interesting mix of content that should be really good for developing the real reputation of the site. In turn they offer:

1. A genuine history of his industry's development with some unique records.
2. An area that entertains and invites relevant visitor-participation.
3. A unique free resource of relevant images.
4. Unique business intelligence that will fascinate his marketplace.
5. A heart-warming story of human endeavour in difficult times.

All of these ideas seem to us to be irresistible reasons for links to start popping up. Anyone remotely interested in goldfish is going to find Bob's site a source of enormous value and they will be drawn to sharing their discovery with others they know in the industry, or who simply keep goldfish themselves. Bob's pursuit of excellence will therefore start turning into the links that Google must find to fall in love with his site. We like to think of the content becoming so good over time that Bob's site becomes a 'destination' site: a site that links lead to; a site people want to visit. Content that creates a destination has to be called 'destination content', naturally.

Alongside this work, Bob realises that he could improve the core information on his website – the information that currently sells the fish. He decides that he is going to make his goldfish information the best he can find on any pet fish website. It will take a while, but he has the knowledge so he will just get on with it, one fish at a time. Before tackling the improvement of the everyday content on his site, Bob revisits his user demand research to make sure he isn't missing any obvious pockets of demand. This reminds him of the goldfish bowl demand, and he sets out to create some great content to improve the Relevance of his site to goldfish bowls.

As with any content Bob decides to produce for his site, only great-value information on goldfish bowls will do. It is better to be really good on a small number of topics than to spread yourself too thinly and be average on lots. Bob does a bit of research to see what the competition is like, and he's not impressed. He then remembers being taken as a child to the factory of a supplier of bowls to his father's shop, and being fascinated by the processes involved. Bob's goldfish bowl information is going to be awesome compared to the current content populating Google's results.

At this point Bob reflects on the focus of his attention, namely just goldfish, and gets a bit worried about the lack of effort going into further information about koi, in particular, and tropical and aquarium fish in general. Bob isn't a koi expert, and knows that it will take years to become one, so we talk about pursuing excellence again and are reassured when we review the volumes of search activity around goldfish. We decide that Bob should aim to be the best in the goldfish niche first and then work sideways into related areas, only when he is confident he can reach the ceiling as the most useful goldfish site on the web.

Building a site with great-value destination content must be the number one objective of any site owner trying to acquire Google's love, but it doesn't mean that destination content always has to have lots of brand new words and valuable editorial that is often hard or expensive to produce, or is dependent on a unique history that is the reserve of the very few. Destination content can also be services or applications, as long as their provision is also a pursuit of excellence. YouTube, for example, now owned by Google, began life as the best website for uploading and sharing video content the web had ever seen. It wasn't words that convinced people to visit it and link to it, it simply did its job better than any other site, even better than Google's own video offering[1] which was online at the same time, and its value to users made its Reputation development unstoppable.

When trying to come up with ideas about how else to build great content, other than words, we suggest you go to Google and start looking at the sites that are performing well in your marketplace. We avoided this exercise at the beginning of this chapter, but now is the time to cast the net wider. Look at your user demand analysis, throw some of the important trends at Google and see what turns up. When the sites in the results aren't competitors, visit them, have a good look around and ask yourself 'What would it take for this site to link to mine?' Often the answer may still be editorial content (yeah, more words), but you will also hit upon ideas that are less dependent on writing. You're interested in sites that aren't competitors, because there is no point trying to get your competitors to link to your site. Sites that aren't competitors, but that perform well for your demand terms, are already basking in the glory of Google's love, so links from them are going to be really influential in Google's view of your site.

Bob is doing this, and the first thing he notices is videos. The Google results show videos from sites that offer practical advice on caring for goldfish. Bob hadn't thought about videos before, so he makes a note to investigate what it will take to produce some for his site that he can also share on these established video sites, so that people will hear about his site through them.

Bob then notices the Wikipedia article on goldfish and wonders what it would take to get his site mentioned in the list of references. He decides that his current content plans may well be sufficient to get a mention, so he makes a note to look into getting it onto the article when it is all ready.

---

[1] http://video.google.com

Sadly for Bob, and everyone else referenced on Wikipedia, no Reputation flows from Wikipedia to the sites it links to. Wikipedia has set its website up in such a way that all the links out of the site carry an attribute that says 'nofollow'[1] – see section 4.2.5 for further details – which means that all the great Reputation that Wikipedia has amassed is not being shared with the rest of the web. Although this seems selfish, the owners have done it to control the way content is added to its encyclopedia. Wikipedia has always been a community resource that anyone can add content to, which meant that as it grew in influence and authority, spammy people couldn't resist putting articles up about their organisations – articles that really didn't warrant an encyclopedia entry – in order to enjoy the flow of Reputation. This 'nofollow' way of managing Reputation flow happens on many sites where users are able to add content, including links to other people's websites.

The next thing Bob notices on an aquatic community site is an advert for an aquarium screensaver. Bob has known for a while that virtual goldfish can be a substitute for the real thing, and he has sold aquarium videos and DVDs for years. He hasn't a clue how to produce a screensaver, but we suggest that he sets up a webcam in the shop pointing at his favourite aquarium where his most beautiful varieties are kept. He'll make sure that when people click on it on his website, it will open up a small dedicated browser window so that they can keep it running in the corner of their computer screen.

---

[1] This is an instruction to Google not to allow the Reputation from the site to follow the link out. Site owners are encouraged to use nofollow when for any reason they are not happy to vote for a site that they otherwise want to link to. For further information: http://www.google.com/support/webmasters/bin/answer.py?hl=en&answer=96569 .

Browsing in your marketplace, looking at the sites that Google thinks are useful to searchers, is time well spent. There is also absolutely nothing wrong with looking at other people's ideas and deciding you can do them better, pursuing excellence all the way. The bottom line again is, if you wouldn't link to it you cannot expect anyone else to. Destination content – that head-turning, great-value information that is irresistible to your marketplace – is your objective, be it small, medium or large in scale and ambition.

4.2.2 Flirting with Tactical Content

Building the best site you possibly can has to be the main objective of your pursuit of a real reputation, but there can be plenty of opportunities to flirt with Google along the way. Before trying to catch Google's eye, refer back to your research about the way people search for the things you do or sell and look for demand that you can dress up into something attractive. We know that sounds a bit superficial, and well, yes, sometimes it is. This isn't a problem, because it's not an exercise in longevity, it is part of the dance with Google that can be effective in keeping your site in its thoughts. So what sort of dressing up do we have in mind? There is an SEO industry term that, while being a bit brutal, does sum it up rather well: link bait[1].

Our love metaphor is being stretched to breaking point here, because you will not be flirting directly with Google if you start link baiting, you will be attempting to impress your peers, in the hope that they will go and tell Google, who is sitting quietly in the corner scanning the room, that you are a great catch.

Link bait has to meet a quality standard to stand a chance of impressing your peers, which means, even though your dressing up isn't how you normally look, you have to stand out as a

---

[1] A Google search on the term will provide you with hours of diversion. Warning: a lot of it is very 'industry-insider'.

something a bit special or it won't actually work. Remember that the point of the exercise is to improve the Reputation of your site. You are baiting links from sites that – on the whole – will be improving your Reputation if they link to yours, and 'special' means your site must hit one or more of these sorts of targets:

- it is genuinely fascinating;
- it sparks controversy;
- it is remarkably quirky;
- it is really insightful;
- it is of the moment;
- it is profoundly useful;
- it is extraordinary;
- it is hysterically funny.

And it must NOT MISS this one:

- it is relevant.

Bob thinks this exercise sounds fun, but he is not a little anxious about whether he is up to the task. Together we refer to the user demand analysis to look at where the trends in goldfish-related searches suggest to start, and here are some of the ideas we come up with:

- 'Goldfish' is the name of a credit and loyalty card brand in the UK from Barclaycard, so Bob is going to offer special discounts and incentives to customers who buy goldfish with Goldfish.
- Appalled by the continuing initiation ritual of goldfish-swallowing in university student bodies around the world, Bob is going to write a detailed piece, with diagrams, about the distress and suffering experienced by the fish when swallowed, in an attempt to discourage this practice.

- The short memory span of goldfish is the stuff of legend – well, myth – and Bob knows that this is nonsense, so he decides to pull together a page debunking it. It turns out that there are a number of academic papers and other popular deconstructions of the myth, so Bob's article will cover them all in detail.
- Some people have a genuine interest in eating goldfish – not swallowing them whole, live, but actually cooking them – but Bob can't quite bring himself to produce recipes, despite the controversy it may spark and the links it may get.
- Bob found over 40 songs listed with 'goldfish' in the title when hunting on iTunes, Napster and Spotify[1] so he is going to create a summary page for them including a brief review of each. He is intending to link each review to somewhere his visitors will be able to buy the songs, hoping he'll earn a few affiliate dollars in the process.
- Demand for information about health and diseases of goldfish – and about dead goldfish – is, er, healthy, so Bob decides to open an online clinic for his visitors, where they can send in photos of their sick or dead fish and Bob will try to work out what's wrong with them or what killed them. Each photo will be published on the site along with Bob's diagnosis. Bob is worried that a gallery of sick and dead fish is not exactly the image he wants people to have of his shop, but he decides to go ahead anyway, confident that it will be genuinely useful and will drive links.

Bob sanity-checks whether these ideas all meet the Relevance standard, and although some will attract links from sites that have very little to do with pet fish, they will always end up

---

[1] http://www.apple.com/itunes/; http://www.napster.com/; http://www.spotify.com/

referring to 'goldfish' in some way in the anchor text, so he is happy. He then schedules the time needed for these link bait exercises in between the time he is spending on his destination content work, which means the next 12 months is pretty well booked up now. Some parts of the link bait work will be quick to implement, so Bob is keen to get these up and working for the site. The others can take their time in the queue for his attention.

If you want a conventional marketing metaphor for link bait, it is nothing more than smart public-relations work for the internet era: snippets of value and interest presented to a marketplace to enhance the reputation of an organisation. For Google's love to be affected by such activities, link bait has to be 'real', meeting demand in a market with genuine, if sometimes controversial, value. Otherwise, Google will not be interested, because bait that is not real will not be taken.

If you fancy entering your link bait into a brutal popularity contest, submit it to Fark, Digg and Reddit. Links from these news and bookmarking services are more directly useful for sites that make their money from visitors, rather than sales, but it does get your name out there. Look at articles that are listed on the home pages of those sites and learn from their structure and style. Topical, ephemeral, exciting, loud, controversial, funny or bizarre stories do well, and can result in large numbers of visitors.

Bob's background, experience and knowledge were great assets in the production of these ideas for both destination content – which will bring people back time and again to his site – and tactical content – which will help introduce people to his website for the first time. Whatever the scale of your opportunities for producing great content for your site, they have to be of a similar nature; they need to make your site a destination for people – who are your prospective customers, after all – seeking useful content in your marketplace. It is also perfectly legitimate to appeal to your users' more ephemeral interests by the more quirky things that you may be up to, or can pull together for their entertainment. The combination of destination and tactical content will produce the sort of value that the sites with authority in your marketplace will come to appreciate, and it is these sites that have the power to affect your Reputation by linking to you. It is the links from these authority sites, more than any others in your market, that you are aiming for, because it doesn't take very many of them to have a positive impact on your Reputation – they are very choosy about who they will link to.

4.2.3 Getting the Word Out: Your Social Media Life

Earlier in this chapter we suggested that Bob had three main advantages that he could bring to bear on his pursuit of a real reputation. The first two, history and knowledge, have been explored in the previous sections; the third was enthusiasm.

Building a real reputation demands energetic participation in your market, and fortunately Bob is no shrinking violet. How you behave online, as in most areas of your life, will determine the success you enjoy, and pursuing Google's love is no different. When it comes to the building of a real reputation, online behaviour comes into its own, because you can be very interactive with your prospective and existing customers and with opinion-formers across your market. This will provide you with countless opportunities to demonstrate your knowledge and integrity, crucial facets of a real reputation. So what does this online best behaviour look like?

In section 4.1.2 Word-of-Mouth Drives Linking we said we would tell you more about acquiring links through word-of-mouth; well, this is where it starts. We like to think of the websites or web services that support online word-of-mouth taking three main forms:

1. They support conversations between individuals and within groups.
2. They enable social groups to meet and share.

3. They share interesting sites and articles within communities with similar interests.

Collectively these sites and services are now known as 'social media' and they take the form of:

1. Instant messaging applications, forums on websites and status updates, such as Messenger, Skype and Twitter.
2. Social networking[1] sites such as MySpace, Bebo and Facebook.
3. Social bookmarking[2] sites such as StumbleUpon, Delicious, Reddit and Digg.

Within each of these environments ordinary people are sharing stuff about their lives and communicating with their friends, family, work colleagues and, increasingly, complete strangers. The rules of engagement within each environment are pretty relaxed until you start trying to push something too hard. People attempting to infiltrate online social groups in order to subsequently sell things or ideas to them are not tolerated; the collective displeasure that is then aimed at such participants can be unpleasant to watch. That said, such reactions should not put you off getting involved, because you are there to build a real reputation, not to flog stuff[3]. Ultimately your activity and behaviour within social media – for the purposes of encouraging visits and the development of Reputation for your site – should reflect the needs of your visitors, particularly when it comes to the nature and the frequency of your communications. Bob's business has frequent contact points with its customers as they purchase new fish food and monitor the health of their fish, so frequent contact is to be expected, but this wouldn't be the case for a washing-machine manufacturer.

---

[1] http://en.wikipedia.org/wiki/Social_network_services
[2] http://en.wikipedia.org/wiki/Social_bookmarking
[3] Well, not directly, at least.

Real Reputation from Being Great to Talk to

Online conversations happen everywhere, so here are some ideas about how to engage with them, in a 'real' way. The first thing you need to do is find the conversations that are relevant to what you do, and there is no better way to do that than by using Google to search for forums and going on Twitter to see what's being said.

Forums – Talk, Talk, Talk

Bob searches on Google for 'forum' along with 'goldfish', 'pet fish', 'fish', 'koi', 'aquarium' and a whole bunch of other related terms and is astonished by the number he finds. He then goes to each, registers his Bob Spetfish username and has a quick look around to see what sort of conversations are going on that he might be able to contribute to. The choice is almost over-whelming. Bob could spend all day every day just discussing goldfish-related topics with the people out there who keep them and want help and advice. The great news is that there are plenty of places he can demonstrate his knowledge and expertise, so he will choose carefully the sites that appear to involve largely British audiences and will make a start on some reputation-building.

Bob's approach is appropriate for most organisations: find the relevant conversations and get stuck in with an identifiable and findable user name. Do not sell, just exude usefulness and start building the real reputation that reflects your ambitions and operations.

Twitter – Follow a Star

At the time of writing (late 2009), Twitter has been in the mainstream for six months. It is in the news everywhere and celebrities are all over it. By the time you read this, it will either have taken over the western hemisphere, been bought by

Google, or be on the wane like many online phenomena, such as MySpace. What Twitter is definitely doing is engaging people all over the world in a type of public conversation that is quite unlike anything seen before. Here is not the place to try and explain why Twitter has caught the public's imagination, the simple fact is that it has and in doing so has provided another great way of getting a real reputation under the noses of many prospective customers of your website.

Bob rushes onto the Twitter website and registers his @bobspetfish user name; good, it's available. He then does a search for references to 'goldfish' to see what sort of activity there is around his area of expertise and finds a constant stream of references to them. He also sees that lots of people are talking about 'twit' being a name for a pregnant goldfish. Bob knows this isn't true and wishes he had some followers to tell. Bob decides to get some interesting updates onto his Twitter account before he starts following the people who are talking about goldfish, so that when they check him out, they will find really useful stuff which should make them more likely to follow him.

After a few weeks, Bob has a fascinating stream of information and status updates on his Twitter account, both about what he's up to with the content he is preparing for his site – a kind of micro-blog which often references his real blog – and about caring for and choosing fish. Bob now has enough information to attract other Twitter users if they should look at his site. On the day Bob decides to start following other people talking about goldfish, he looks at what today's stream of conversation is saying about goldfish and writes a few responses to them. Bob then spends the rest of the afternoon following everyone he can find who has mentioned goldfish recently. And to his delight most of them follow him back.

This is just the beginning of Bob's use of Twitter to build a real reputation, but the foundations are in place, and as long as he uses it only to demonstrate why he is worth knowing, his reputation will start to build.

Bob wonders at first how to make himself available to instant messaging, when he doesn't want to be available all the time to everyone. So instead he signs up to Skype and connects his availability status to his website and allows a Friday chat to take place every week for an hour, where he runs a live clinic for visitors to ask him questions about their fish. He hasn't decided whether to do this with video yet.

Social Networking – Come Over to My Place

On Facebook Bob searches for all groups that are specifically about goldfish and pet fish and joins all the ones that look as if they have active members and interesting conversations. Sometimes, when seeing how much enthusiasm some people muster around the creatures he is so invested in, Bob forgets he has to sell goldfish to make a living. Participating in social networks about goldfish is hardly work – which reminds him he mustn't neglect his other duties as he has heard of people becoming addicted to social networking.

Bob decides that Bebo's audience is too young to be able to get directly involved with; he'd feel a bit creepy approaching the kids on Bebo to be their friends, just so that he can talk about their goldfish. And likewise MySpace just doesn't feel like the right environment for what he knows and what he's about. So Bob decides to focus the energies he can spare on working on Facebook.

Similar conditions may surround your use of social networking sites, and you may find business-oriented networks like LinkedIn to be a more appropriate place to get involved. The principles of your involvement, though, are identical: sell nothing and build a real reputation for what you know and what you can do.

Social Bookmarking – Delicious Stumbling

Social bookmarking can be very effective in driving awareness of sites, particularly if as a bookmarker you develop a real reputation for linking to the best sites in your area of interest. Bookmark informative articles on your chosen topics in Delicious (or Furl, or Google Bookmark if you prefer). Again, be useful. You want your list of bookmarks to be an authoritative list of interesting and worthwhile content on your subject – not just on your own site, but across the web.

StumbleUpon is another good place to start. Sign up for an account, download and install the toolbar and you're ready to go. For your own material, submit new pages as soon as you have written them – each time you create a new page, submit the URL to StumbleUpon using the toolbar. This will increase the number of web pages you have in the StumbleUpon database and improve the likelihood of your site being stumbled upon. Carefully select topic titles, and add multiple, accurate tags – this attracts a wide range of users and keeping these as relevant to the content as possible will help to keep the traffic targeted.

This isn't enough. Leave it there, and you're just another social media marketer. You need to have a real involvement in the StumbleUpon / Delicious communities for it to turn into a real reputation. Be useful and knowledgeable in your subject. Don't just bookmark your own material – mark and rate a wide range of worthwhile, informative websites relevant to the subjects your site covers; this helps these websites appear for people who have similar interests to your own, and therefore they will be more likely to find and value your site. Add friends with similar interests – more people will see your newly added web pages. Friends with relevant interests are more likely to give your site the thumbs up. Join relevant StumbleUpon groups and forums.

Bob already has a list of useful sites that he has collected over the years, so he decides to register his name on just StumbleUpon and Delicious for now – after all he is just one man, and there is so much real reputation work to do – and spends another happy afternoon populating his bookmarks and starting some conversations with the other community members; boy, he says to himself, there are some interesting and nice people out there.

4.2.4 Yes, But Is It Real?

Remember it is the goodwill that comes from your engagement with these word-of-mouth engines that turns into relevant links from all sorts of places. It isn't the links themselves that you are after. Often such links are set to stop Google passing love from the site they are appearing on, because otherwise they would be inundated with spam. Links therefore come indirectly from your real reputation, so you will never be sure which bits of your hard work were responsible for the ones that you acquire – a bit like the bad old days of advertising where half of what you spent was wasted, but you never knew which half.

One of the most effective ways of assessing whether your marketplace believes you are a genuine and valuable member of it is to take the plunge and run a customer forum on your own website. Here you will really find whether your reputation is as spotless as you'd like to think it is. As we said earlier in this chapter, real reputation is for the courageous, and there is no greater organisational courage online than allowing your customers to comment directly on your website, in public, about you. Before setting off down this road, however, it is probably a good idea if you first get a handle on the general state of your customer service relationships, as you may be in for a bit of a shock. Don't overreact to this, but hold onto the ambition: show your customers how determined you are to improve everything about your organisation and engage them in a meaningful, real, way.

Bob has decided that he is definitely going to run a forum on his own site, because it would be great if people started to say nice things about him for other customers to see. He knows that his record with his current customers is impeccable, so he has no fear that anything they say might put off other customers. In fact he realises that by allowing the forum to grow over time, it will start to contribute to the Relevance of the site as users start to produce questions and answers of their own. Bob learns that these questions and answers become content that the SEO industry calls user-generated, which is really cheap to produce – in other words, free – and always likely to be relevant to demand, because the people expressing the demand are also producing the content.

4.2.5 Sharing the Love – Linking to the Sites You Love (and Don't)

Sharing Love Is Real

For a search engine that depends on the links between sites to make sense of the world's information, a few carefully chosen links out of your site to the sites you 'love' are the done thing and feed for Google's voracious appetite for assessing the Reputation of sites on the web. Don't be afraid to do it, and don't try and keep your Reputation all to yourself by linking to no-one. What goes around comes around, and users of the web thrive on following links from sites they trust to sites that those sites trust, growing their regard for all these sites as they do so. By showing other site owners that you are happy to link to valuable sources yourself, you will encourage them to link to your site.

Reciprocate Intelligently

Google's view of links from sites that point to each other will be determined by their individual qualities, namely the Reputation each source site (and source URL) has in Google's eyes. Because no two links will ever be exactly equal in these terms they will contribute their Reputation value in both directions, but on different criteria, based on their differing levels of authority and Relevance. Google cannot know if these links are pre-arranged, and they frequently occur in a perfectly legitimate manner, so there is no recommendation to avoid them. As a consequence, you shouldn't be afraid to link to a site that links to yours – in a misplaced fear that it might cancel out the good their link does – but you must do it for the right reason, namely because their site has quality content that will be useful to your visitors. If their site is not relevant to yours, or if their content is of dubious quality, don't do it. Irrelevant links will flag to Google that you are a possible link-sharer, which may result in your site being penalised in some way.

There are reciprocal linking plans and link exchanges provided by third-party businesses who are attempting to manipulate Google's perception of the sites included, but most of these will involve far too many irrelevant sites and therefore should be avoided. Google itself has a name for groups of linking sites like these; it refers to them as bad neighbourhoods. You really want to avoid acquiring links from anything that Google might consider to be a bad neighbourhood.

There may also be occasions when you want to link to a site from your site, but for one reason or another – perhaps it's a negative story about a competitor – you don't want the link to pass any of your Reputation over. In this situation you can add an attribute to the link code that says rel="nofollow", which tells Google not to allow the Reputation to flow between the two sites. Here is an example of how to place the attribute in the link code: <a href="http://www.example.com/" rel="nofollow">No.1 in Google Guaranteed</a>.

4.3 PRACTICAL LINK NURTURING

Online Reputation is the most important factor in when it comes to generating high levels of search traffic from Google. To obtain it – as you well know by now – your site has to be linked to from sites which are considered authoritative[1] in your subject area. This is hard. If you get one good editorial link

---

[1] How do you know if they're authoritative? They rank well in Google for relevant terms in your market.

from a site dealing with your subject area after a few days of work, you're doing well.

Don't be depressed: we've worked with top-ranking sites in competitive sectors that have huge marketing budgets but only have around 100 decent links to their site. A typical niche area can rank well with perhaps ten. The first links are the hardest. After that there's a feedback loop – the more people link, the more people find your site, the more people link, and so on.

4.3.1 Showing the Way

Once you've done your bit at spreading the word (and it's a long-term commitment), you can also think about reminding other people to share your site out there too. We would suggest putting buttons at the base of any informative articles (or products, if interesting) on your web pages to allow others to share them. Don't go nuts. We've seen some articles with 30 little icons after them, begging readers to click on them. We'd just stick with three or four of your favourites, perhaps StumbleUpon (as it's great), Delicious (as it's been around a while), Facebook (popular) and Twitter (ditto). Digg and Reddit might be nice for news stories only (you are submitting them to Google News, aren't you? You aren't?[1]). Oh, and email – that's real word of mouth – email people telling them what you are up to.

4.3.2 Encourage Day-to-Day Linking by Invitation

While the content of third-party sites and their links are hard to control, you must try to influence the anchor text of the links your site acquires. One way of achieving this is simply to ask those people visiting to create links in a suggested format as provided by your own pages. Ask them to refer to the target site in a particular way, then make it easy for them to do so by

---

[1] See section 5.1.5 Telling Google about Collections of Pages for further details.

providing the HTML they require. Give visitors snippets of HTML that include the URLs to link to and, crucially, the anchor text that is preferred.

Produce a short piece of content that suggests that if people have found the site or content useful, a link from their site could help other users find it. Encourage them to use particular types of relevant vocabulary or short descriptions about the target site – these can be provided in a number of literal forms – so that the chance of good link context increases. And, finally, give them explicit permission to link to your site.

4.3.3 Use RSS Feeds to Package Content and Links

RSS (Really Simple Syndication) feeds are an effective way of releasing content from your site with embedded links back to your site. The willingness of others to use such feeds as content for their sites, including your links, will clearly depend on how useful and relevant it is to them. If your content is suitable, this can be an effective means of building links that are in your direct control. Don't give away the family silver in your feeds though. Carefully select sections of your pages, or abstracted articles, that will make a visit to your site much more likely and not just provide free content for other sites, which may simply make a visit to your site redundant.

4.3.4 Links from Reputation Authorities

Both generally and within your market there will be sites that command significant amounts of authority, from which links are Reputation-heavy and highly prized. Appearing in links from these sites is a foundation issue for your site and is usually indispensable for any organisation needing to be taken seriously by Google. There are two types of authority sites: general and specific, and below are some examples.

General Authority: The Open Directory Project[1]

As 'the largest human-edited directory on the web' the Open Directory Project (ODP) has a history of being taken very seriously by Google and is used as a feed into Google's own directory[2] service. The ODP is a general authority site which has a double dose of credibility, as far as Google is concerned, because all of its editors are volunteers. While this is presumed to ensure that the content is highly accurate and valuable, submitting a site for inclusion in the ODP is an essential step in your journey to acquire some valuable Reputation early on. The application process is straightforward; the arrival of the subsequent link, however, happens somewhat inconsistently. Being volunteers, busy section editors can be known to take months to add a new entry. The ODP data itself is available under licence, and is frequently syndicated around the web; however, these syndicated links are of little value from a Reputation point-of-view because the data is recognised as a duplication of the ODP. Because you are dealing with volunteer editors, we recommend that you follow these important rules when submitting your site to the ODP:

1. Never lose patience with an ODP editor as there are no rights of entry.
2. Never submit a site for inclusion before it is ready.
3. Read the rules[3].

General Authority: The Yahoo Directory[4]

The Yahoo Directory is also a general authority site and was the first directory of its kind. It retains a global influence as a long-standing, paid-entry directory and its authority and reliability make it a useful source for Google when it seeks confirmation

---

1 http://dmoz.org/
2 http://directory.google.com/
3 http://www.dmoz.org/add.html
4 http://search.yahoo.com/dir

of a site's Relevance to a particular marketplace. Entry in the Yahoo Directory attracts an annual fee, but typically this is a trivial cost to most organisations. As with the ODP, the Yahoo Directory appears around the web, not under licence but under Yahoo's own regional domain locations. Links are flat (i.e. simple hypertext links in HTML) and pass Reputation only from the category listings of sites, not from search results pages on which your site may also appear.

Specific Authority: Industry or Market Authorities

Every industry or market sector has its share of specific über-authority sites, which are not always competitors. Such sites must be located and targeted for special treatment in the securing of Reputation; for example, professional bodies, trade associations and specialist press fit this particular description. Frequently, as with Yahoo, these sites charge fees for placing links, but typically, if the link is simple and visible with the anchor text under the submitter's control, such payment can be well worth it. Better still, if they are free, then a simple request achieves the same end. Scrutiny of paid links, however, is an area of much activity for Google's anti-spam initiatives – because paying for Reputation can be effective but not real, but Google can struggle to spot the impostor – so it is far better to become irresistible to such sites than have to approach them or pay for the link.

Bob is very interested in finding the authority sites in his sector to see if he can do anything in particular that might make them want to link to him. The problem is that he isn't sure how to find them. He then remembers that when working through his content ideas, he used Google to research sites and the sorts of content they were producing. Turning to Google again, Bob starts looking for authority sites in the pet fish sector. He decides that, for now, he is going to focus on goldfish, so simply types this word in and looks through the results.

The first result he comes across is Wikipedia. He's encountered the goldfish article on Wikipedia more times than he's had hot dinners, but despite the general authority of the site and the specific authority of this article, Bob knows that Reputation doesn't flow from Wikipedia, because of the nofollow attribute. What does dawn on him, though, thinking again about his real reputation, is that he can start contributing to this and all the other goldfish articles. So he registers at Wikipedia as Bob Spetfish, and makes a note to himself to start uploading some of his grandfather's photos as a first step. With 'Bob Spetfish' starting to appear in the list of contributors, the other goldfish experts will look him up and find his site; this can only be good for the chances of being linked to.

Thinking about Wikipedia further, Bob reckons his great-grandfather is an interesting enough historical figure for Bob to put up a mini-biography of him on the site and for it not to be seen as a stunt for a commercial site. If he is successful, he may then be able to link from the article to his site as the business his ancestor established, which will increase awareness of the site.

Moving on, Bob takes another look at the Google results. In the top ten results in the UK[1] there is only one other likely specialist authority that isn't a competitor. The rest are results for the credit card, a bunch of general links to videos and some news stories on general newspaper sites. The one with potential is the website of the UK's best-selling fishkeeping magazine, *Practical Fishkeeping*, which must therefore become a target for a link. Bob sees a regular 'Website of the Week' feature and decides he will submit his site, once all the destination content is live. He also notices on the magazine site a list of clubs and associations around the country. None of these club websites appeared in Google's first pages of results for a 'goldfish' search, but Bob reckons that, in their way, they will be little pockets of Reputation that could be quite easily secured if he makes the right approach. His idea is simple: if members of the clubs mention their affiliation to the club when they purchase from

1 At noon, 30 November 2009, to be precise.

him, he will offer them a discount. This isn't a particularly great idea, Bob concedes, but it will be simple to implement and may make a bit of a difference.

In view of all Bob's other commitments, he decides to come back to his hunt for authority sites at a later date, and will probably start with more specific searches to generate different lists of sites. And besides, he has his ODP and Yahoo directory entries to get on with.

These practical steps towards kick-starting and encouraging links to your site conclude our look at how to build Reputation for your site. And this also concludes the chapters of the book where we have been explaining how to identify and pursue the Relevance and Reputation you will need to build a Tripod of Love. We are now moving on to look at how to assemble the Visibility leg of your Tripod of Love. It is unavoidable that we get technical from this point on. Websites are built on hardware, software and networks, and Google is a giant technology beast. We have to talk about the practical technology issues of building a visible site for Google at some point, and this is it.

50 WAYS . . .

11. Your majority shareholder/stakeholder needs to understand the importance of Google and how on-line excellence builds Reputation. So start talking to them today.

12. Do not assume that the existence of your site is enough for other sites to link to it. Take a hard look at your market and commit to being better online than the rest of it. *See section 4.1.1*

13. Spend time, not money, encouraging the world to talk about you online. People talking about your website is better than having a big marketing budget. *See section 4.1.2*

14. Make sure your URLs are not a mess of duplicates that dilute the power of links, because Reputation links are to URLs, not to pages. *See section 4.1.3*

15. If in doubt about what your Reputation should look like, go back to basics, be courageous, and build a real reputation around who you are and what you do. *See section 4.2*

16. Be prepared to create content worthy of a destination website – deeper, richer, more complete and simply better than your competitors – if you want the links a destination deserves. *See section 4.2.1*

17. Develop tactical Reputation (link bait) content as long as it's funny or controversial or insightful or quirky or genuinely fascinating, but most of all Relevant! *See section 4.2.2*

18. Get the word out about your wonderful website by participating in the social media conversations that are relevant to it. Be brave, honest and helpful, and avoid direct sales! *See section 4.2.3*

19. Online status updates and social groups are powerful ways of spreading the word about your site, so use them regularly and intelligently. This means sanity-checking their likely Relevance and making sure their frequency is appropriate for the behaviours in your market. *See section 4.2.3*

20. Share your knowledge and experience; become an expert in your sector; do not waffle and divert. Stay focused and always be useful and relevant; the rest will take care of itself. *See section 4.2.3*

21. Don't be afraid to link to the sites that you love and that may be useful to your visitors. Being really useful is a great way to acquire Reputation. *See section 4.2.5*

22. Suggest to your visitors that they link to you if they find your site useful. Make it easy for them with snippets of HTML. *See section 4.3*
23. Submit your site for inclusion in the Open Directory Project and buy your standard entry in the Yahoo Directory. *See section 4.3.4*
24. Find the authority sites in your sector and develop strategies to make a link from them to you irresistible. All sectors have their pockets of powerful and relevant authority; find them and get planning. *See section 4.3.4*

5

BUILD YOUR WEBSITE FOR GOOGLE

5.1 STRUCTURING FOR GOOGLE

Entropy is the absence of structure, the absence of information. Entropy is meaninglessness. We don't like entropy. We are big fans of meaning.

Start with raw data, add structure to turn it into information, add a mind to make it into knowledge – perhaps even action. The quality of the eventual knowledge, however, relies on the amount of information that can be added to the data through structure. Google relies on structure too, to understand the relative importance and relationships between the different phrases and thematic vocabulary in a page.

Websites are mostly composed of pages of text. Any phrase in the text can be anchored to another page held anywhere on the web, providing a link that can be followed by the user. This organisation of pages anchored to phrases is beyond plain text – it is 'hypertext'. Like text, but more so.

These pages of hypertext also contain special marks for software (such as a web browser, or Google) to determine the purpose of each part of the text. These marks are called 'tags' – usually one at the beginning of a phrase, sentence, paragraph or block to be marked up, and another at the end. A system of tags to mark up hypertext needed a snappy name. No one came up with one, so we're stuck with HyperText Markup Language, or HTML[1].

---

[1] We tend to use an extension of HTML nowadays that imposes cleaner structure – Extensible HyperText Markup Language, or XHTML.

The best[1] HTML does the following:

- Adds meaning to the text. HTML can make clear to Google the meaning or importance of various chunks of text. Google will use this information when calculating the Relevance of your page to search terms.
- Doesn't add anything else. Font sizes, typefaces, colours, layout and other styling should be held in a separate stylesheet file. This separation of style from content makes the remaining HTML compact and easy for Google to read.

Let's just look at the most common pieces of hypertext markup, and what they tell Googlebot – and big Momma Google – about the text they surround.

5.1.1 Telling Google about Phrases and Sentences

Google lives in a world of interrelated phrases. Here are a few of the most important ways in which you can use markup to give Google more information about a word, a phrase, a sentence, or any combination of these (we'll assume from here on that 'phrase' covers any string of text shorter than a paragraph).

Emphasised and Strongly Emphasised
These markup tags denote a phrase that you think is more important than the surrounding text. Text marked as emphasised

---

[1] You can determine the general quality of the mark-up on a page using the W3C validator (http://validator.w3.org). Quality mark-up abides by such standard practices as separation of text content and its styling, and is very important for people with disabilities. Google itself can usefully be thought of as the most prolific blind, mouse-less user of the web. A detailed set of guidelines on the art of making web pages accessible to blind, mouse-less users (and plenty more besides) is published by the W3C, and are available at http://www.w3.org/TR/WCAG20/. Following these web content accessibility guidelines is pretty much a basic requirement of optimising a site for Google.

is typically shown visually by using *italics*[1], and text marked as strongly emphasised as **emboldened text**.

Googlebot wants to know what you think is the most important part of a sentence. To mark a phrase as emphasised, use *the em tag*. To mark a phrase as strongly emphasised, use **the strong tag**.

Of course, this is handy for humans too – when they look at a web page they often skim through for words that jump out at them – 'scenting information', before bothering to read it fully. They may never even read the whole page, just pull out the part that seems the most relevant to their needs and then click off to somewhere else.

Of course, if everything on the page were bold, nothing would stand out as more important than the rest – and the same applies for Google. Emphasis, then, should be used sparingly for best effect.

Abbreviations and Acronyms

Some words are abbreviations for other words. For example, 'St' can be either 'Saint' or 'Street', depending on the context.

An acronym is a word made up of the first letters of other words that serves as an abbreviation for those words. For example, NASA is a word (pronounced 'nassa' rather than 'en ay ess ay') and therefore an acronym.

BBC, however, is an abbreviation. If you find yourself nodding furiously in agreement, well done, as abbreviations and acronyms are marked up differently in HTML.

---

[1] Actually it's technically usually an 'oblique' (slanted) version of the font, rather than actual italics. But people tend to call oblique italic anyway. Indeed, in early versions of HTML these emphasised and strongly emphasised elements were marked as <i>italic</i> and bold. This was abandoned in favour of referring to the structural intent (emphasised and strongly emphasised) rather than the typographic style that implied it. So remember, in HTML be strong, not bold!

Google wants to know what words you have hiding behind those abbreviations and acronyms. To mark up an abbreviation, use the `<abbr title="abbreviation">abbr</abbr>` tag. To mark up an acronym, `<acronym title="use the acronym tag">UTAT</acronym>`. Don't do it for every occurrence of the abbreviation or acronym on the page, just the first one.

Humans may also be interested. If you are using a mouse, hovering over an acronym or abbreviation will reveal its 'title' attribute, if it has one.

Quoted Phrases

You will occasionally want to quote text that appears somewhere else, or that has been said by someone else.

Google is very interested to know if you are referring in some way to a quote. It is also interested in where that quote came from – it is a link of sorts, even if no hyperlink is provided – so you can give a citation for the quote.

To mark up a quoted phrase as part of another sentence use `<q cite="http://www.searchjohnston.co.uk/quoting-text">the q tag</q>`[1]. The cite attribute is optional, and doesn't have to be a web address – it could just be someone's name.

Other Phrases that Can Be Marked Up[2]

A few more bits of phrasal markup, just for the sake of completeness. These aren't used as often, but still convey handy information.

---

[1] Different browsers treat this tag in different ways. For example, some insert quote marks around text marked up with it. This can be annoying if you have put quote marks in the text yourself. You can resolve this simply by avoiding quote marks in quoted phrases and visually styling the quoted phrases as italic.

[2] There are a few more tags not listed here. If you are writing about computer code, code fragments are marked using `<code>`, sample output from the program are marked using `<samp>`. Text to be entered via the keyboard is marked using `<kbd>`, and variables or arguments can be marked using `<var>`. For those wishing to show edits to documents, inserted text is marked using `<ins>` and deleted text using `<del>`. There are also a few 'whitespace' elements that can be marked up, such as line breaks `<br />` and horizontal rules `<hr />`.

- Citation (`<cite>cite tags</cite>`), used to denote a citation or reference to other sources. It often contains a link. If you refer to information without actually quoting directly, this is how to do it.
- Superscript (`<sup>sup tags</sup>`) and subscript (`<sub>sub tags</sub>`), handy if you want to talk about areas (m^2) rather than motorways (M2), or very big numbers such as 10^{32} rather than somewhat smaller numbers such as 1032. Or indeed imaginary chemicals such as B_{52} rather than real bombers such as the B52.
- Definition (`<dfn>dfn tags</dfn>`), which denotes the defining instance of the enclosed term. You are pretty unlikely to use this one. We think it may be for showing off in scientific literature.

Images

Images are often served as results in the main Google results pages, and Google Image Search is around 4.35% of Google's search visits[1], so they are worth consideration.

An image is referenced in HTML like this: `<img src="/images/goldfish-in-bowl.jpg" alt="a goldfish in a bowl" />`.

Images are essentially invisible to Google (so far, though this may change in the future), but their attributes are not. The most important attribute of an image, as far as Google is concerned, is its alternate text description – in the example above it is 'a goldfish in a bowl'[2].

---

[1] Source: Hitwise December 2009

[2] The text you use for an alt attribute should be seen as a textual equivalent of the image – usually this will not be a description of the image itself. For example, if the image is your company logo, the alt attribute should be the name of your company not a description of what your logo looks like. If an image has no value as content but is just there as 'decoration' for the page, you should still include an alt attribute but it should be empty: e.g. `<img src="decoration-image.jpg" alt="" />`. Where possible such 'decoration' images should be referenced in an external stylesheet as backgrounds. This technique avoids the informationally poor image tags appearing in the HTML.

Google also seems to pay some attention to the words in the filename, in this case 'goldfish-in-bowl.jpg', so make the actual filenames of the images on your site as descriptive and as relevant as possible to the page in which they sit.

5.1.2 Telling Google about Blocks of Text

So far we have dealt with markup for phrases, sentences, and fragments and groups thereof. Next comes the structure of the document itself. We can tell Google how one subject moves to the next, group them and show thematic structure, using the relationships between paragraphs, headings and other blocks, as well as larger page divisions.

Paragraphs and Headings

The humble paragraph has been around a long time, and together with its related headings it is perhaps the most important way we have of grouping together concepts for Googlebot's attention. Headings and paragraphs can be arranged to show order and group relationships between them – for example, a heading can be followed by a paragraph, which implies a relationship between the heading and that paragraph.

The paragraph indicates a change of subject, following on from the preceding paragraph, and leading into the succeeding one. In some of the best argumentative writing, sentences offer this conceptual movement too, ever moving the subject forward, perhaps handing it on as an object for the next sentence, perhaps retaining it as the subject. Paragraphs then can offer a larger change in concept. Once you have your paragraphs sorted out, headings can be introduced to highlight the conceptual changes held within the paragraphs, and the relationships of the paragraph concepts to each other. The beginnings of paragraphs are marked up using <p> tags, the ends with </p>.

Headings should be additive, ideally. In a perfect world, they should further describe a conceptual structure that should already be apparent just from reading the paragraphs themselves. HTML offers six levels of heading (tagged using **<h1>** to **<h6>**) that can be used to structure a page, with level 1 being the most important, and level 6 the least.

The relationships between headings are worth some consideration.

<h1> Heading A
  Paragraph 1

  <h2> Heading B
  Paragraph 2
  Paragraph 3

  <h2> Heading C
  Paragraph 4

    <h3> Heading D
    Paragraph 5

      <h4> Heading E
      Paragraph 6

  <h2> Heading F
  Paragraph 7

Here we are telling Google the following things:

- The words in Heading A describe the content of paragraphs 1 through 7.
- The words in Heading B describe the content of paragraphs 2 and 3. It denotes the beginning of a first subsection of Heading A.
- The words in Heading C describe the content of paragraphs 4, 5 and 6. It is as important as Heading B and F. It denotes the beginning of a second subsection of Heading A.
- The words in Heading D describe the content of

paragraphs 5 and 6. It denotes the beginning of a subsection of Heading C.

- The words in Heading E describe the content of paragraph 6. It denotes the beginning of a subsection of Heading D.
- The words in Heading F describe the content of paragraph 7. It is as important as Heading B and C. It denotes the beginning of a third subsection of Heading A.

All this is wonderfully juicy information for Google – as long as you use it properly! If the above tags can be used to tell Google more about your text, the misuse of them can be used to tell it less. The misuse of markup usually comes about when trying to achieve a visual effect. Headings are often misused simply to obtain a particular font size. Such visual effects should be achieved using stylesheets, not markup, to avoid creating unnecessary confusion.

Look again at the heading/paragraph structure above, then consider the following web page 'wireframe' mock-up.

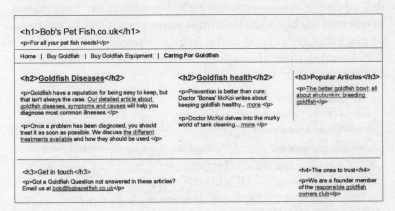

Is Bob's Pet Fish.co.uk really the main focus of this section navigation page? Bob's Pet Fish.co.uk is the name of the *site*, not the main focus of the page. Is 'Popular Articles' really a sub-section of 'Goldfish Diseases'? Is 'The ones to trust' really a subsection of 'Get in touch'? These are the sorts of confusing signals that web pages send out to Google every day.

So how could Bob's page be better structured? A better strategy would be to use a new heading, 'Caring for Goldfish', as the level 1 heading of the page, and leave the 'Bob's Pet Fish.co.uk' logo as ordinary text (or an image). 'Popular Articles' is a handy navigational element, but dilutes the goldfish-care Relevance of the page. A better choice would be 'More on Goldfish' set at heading level 2, with links about other aspects of fish care. If this were done, then the next two headings 'Get in touch' and 'The ones to trust' could be considered as subsections of 'More on Goldfish', and so could both be set at heading level 3. Intelligent use of page divisions (see section 5.1.3 Telling Google about Relationships between Blocks) should then be used to group the main content – including the heading level 1 – separately from the 'More on Goldfish' content. (By the way, Bob should also think about the text he is using for his links. The word 'more' on its own isn't descriptive of the content beneath. Because of the importance of internal anchor text, Bob must make sure his links are from phrases that are related to the linked-to pages).

Bob makes these changes to the wireframe, resulting in:

Bob's Pet Fish.co.uk
<p>For all your pet fish needs!</p>

Home | Buy Goldfish | Buy Goldfish Equipment | **Caring For Goldfish**

<h1>Caring for Goldfish</h1>

<h2>Goldfish Diseases</h2>   **<h2>Goldfish Health</h2>**   <h2>More on Goldfish</h2>

<p>Goldfish have a reputation for being easy to keep, but that isn't always the case. Our detailed article about goldfish diseases, symptoms and causes will help you diagnose most common illnesses. </p>

<p>Once a problem has been diagnosed, you should treat it as soon as possible. We discuss the different treatments available and how they should be used. </p>

<p>Prevention is better than cure; Doctor 'Bones' McKoi writes about keeping goldfish healthy... </p>

<p>Doctor McKoi delves into the murky world of tank cleaning....</p>

<p>The better goldfish bowl; all about shubunkin; breeding goldfish</p>

<h3>Get in touch</h3>   <h3>The ones to trust</h3>

<p>Got a Goldfish Question not answered in these articles? Email us at bob@bobspetfish.co.uk</p>

<p>We are a founder member of the responsible goldfish owners club</p>

Lists

A list is a collection of phrases or sentences, or even (but more rarely) paragraphs. Any sequential set of related items is, essentially, a list. Items in the list are marked up using <li>li (list item) tags</li>. The list items are grouped together as a list. In some, sequential order is important, such as steps in a process, so the list items are grouped as an <ol>ordered list</ol>. In others, order is unimportant, and the list items are grouped as an <ul>unordered list</ul>. In the markup, a list will look something like this list of the members of the 60s pop sensation 'Dave Dee, Dozy, Beaky, Mick and Tich':

```
<ol>
  <li>Dave Dee</li>
  <li>Dozy</li>
  <li>Beaky</li>
  <li>Mick</li>
  <li>Tich</li>
</ol>
```

A list item can contain another list – for example, the navigation menu of a website can be usefully defined as a set of nested lists, such as this list of household chores for pirates:

```
<ul>
  <li>Do washing
    <ol>
      <li>Put dirty clothes in washing machine</li>
      <li>Turn machine on</li>
      <li>When finished, unload clean clothes and hang to dry</li>
    </ol>
  </li>
  <li>Get milk and papers</li>
```

```
<li>Splice mainbrace (again)</li>
<li>Mow lawn</li>
<li>Feed parrot</li>
<li>Polish silver
  <ul>
    <li>Coins</li>
    <li>Plate</li>
    <li>Don't forget to shine hook</li>
  </ul>
</li>
</ul>
```

A third kind of list is a definition list, used for glossaries and similar things. Here there is a surrounding **<dl>** tag, containing terms (**<dt></dt>**) and their definition(s) (**<dd></dd>**). For example:

```
<dl>
  <dt>Bat</dt>
    <dd>Club or stick, often made of wood, used to hit a ball</dd>
    <dd>Small nocturnal flying mammal</dd>
  <dt>Ball</dt>
    <dd>Spherical object, hit with a bat (definition 1)</dd>
</dl>
```

The actual type of list style – round bullets, Roman numerals, lower-case letters and so on – can be defined separately as a style. So in the definition list above, where there were two definitions of the first term, we might want to number them to make it easier to explain which type of bat the ball was to be hit with.

The Best of the Rest: Block Quotes and Tables

When you are quoting a block of text (rather than a phrase) that appears somewhere else, again, Google wants to know. You can tell it using the blockquote tag, again with the optional cite attribute to show exactly where it came from.

```
<blockquote cite="http://www.searchjohnston.co.uk/quoting-text-
blocks"> <p>You may also want to quote a whole block of text –
perhaps several paragraphs, lists and so on. If so, you can use the
blockquote tag.</p></blockquote>
```

Misuses include marking something as a block quote simply to indent it. Such visual effects should be achieved using stylesheets, not markup.

If block quotes have been misused, tables have been positively abused, implemented as ways of laying out a page. Using table markup for page layout is messy, results in bulky, unnecessary markup, and is generally a very bad idea. Layout should be accomplished using an external stylesheet file, not by abusing informational markup. Table markup should only be used for tabulating data into rows and columns. It is useful to highlight to Google which cells are the table column and row headings using table heading tags (<th></th>)[1].

5.1.3 Telling Google about Relationships between Blocks

You will often need to chunk up the page – whether for display purposes, or simply to gather together sections of the page such as navigation, content, links to other information, contact details and so on. The start of a division is marked with a <div> tag, the end with a </div> closure tag. Divisions may be contained in

---

[1] In the case of very complicated tables, there is a raft of mark-up that allows you to show exactly which data cells a heading applies to. This becomes on the whole less important for Google but more important for human users – especially those with disabilities using special access technologies. More information on this can be found at http://www.communis.co.uk/complex-table-mark-up/.

other divisions, to allow further groupings within the page – for example:

```
<div id="top">
   <div id="logo">[logo image goes here]</div>
   <div id="navigationmenu">[list of navigation links goes
   here]</div>
   <div id="contactdetails">[list of contact details goes here]</div>
</div>

<div id="maincontent">
   <h1>[Main Heading goes here]</h1>
   <p>[paragraph goes here]</p>
   <p>[paragraph goes here]</p>
   <div id="boxoutsection">
      <h2>Top tips</h2>
      <p>[paragraph goes here]</p>
   </div>
   <h2>[Subheading goes here]</h2>
   <p>[paragraph goes here]</p>
</div>

<div id="relatedcontent">
   <h2>Related</h2>
   <ul>[list of related pages goes here]</ul>
</div>
```

Note here how the divisions have been used to separate the main page content following the level 1 heading, in the division with the id attribute "maincontent", from the less relevant content held in the division with the id attribute "related content". The id attributes given here are incidental – it's the division structure that gives information, not the identifying names they are given. Discussions are afoot at the W3C[1] and elsewhere about how to formally mark up particular types of block according to purpose (e.g. navigation menus, contact information) using 'role' attributes, which are likely to make an appearance in HTML5.

5.1.4 Telling Google about Whole Pages

Still with us? All that dividing up of pages making your head spin? Well don't worry, it gets a bit simpler for a while, as we move on to discuss how to tell Google about the whole page.

The main body of text held in a HTML page – all those divisions, headings, paragraphs and so on – is preceded by a head section that holds information about the information in the page. It is data about data, so it is called 'metadata'.

A typical head section will contain the following information to be read by any piece of software that's interested:

Actual markup	Translation
`<!DOCTYPE html PUBLIC "-//W3C//DTD XHTML 1.0 Strict//EN" "DTD/xhtml1-strict.dtd">`	*I'm marked up in XHTML, version 1.0, and am sticking strictly to the rules about it.*
`<html xmlns="http://www.w3.org/1999/xhtml" xml:lang="en" lang="en">`	*The HTML proper is starting now. XHTML is just one of many kinds of Extensible Markup Languages; here are some specifics about which flavour I'm using. The text it is marking up is all going to be in English.*

---

[1] W3C (the World Wide Web Consortium) is the de facto international standards body for the web. These are the good people who specify exactly what can be marked up and how. It can take a long time, but is usually worth the wait. See www.w3.org for more.

Actual markup	Translation
`<head>`	*I am starting the 'head' section, containing all the metadata – this is information about the information in the page below.*
`<title>How To Look After Goldfish</title>`	*This page is titled 'How To Look After Goldfish'.*
`<meta name="description" content="A detailed look at ways to do your best for your Goldfish including health, habitat, food, cleaning and plenty more besides" />`	*I would like its description to someone viewing search results to be 'A detailed look at ways to do your best for your Goldfish including health, habitat, food, cleaning and plenty more besides'.*
`<link rel="stylesheet" type="text/css" media="all" href="style.css" />`	*Please load the styling and layout for this page on all media (print, handheld, on-screen) from the cascading stylesheet file style.css.*
`<script src="scripts.js" type="text/javascript" />`	*There are some scripts I want to load for some neat additive interactions at scripts.js.*
`</head>`	*OK, that's the end of the head section. On to the body next!*

The words with which you title the page – marked up using the `<title>`title tag`</title>` – do not appear in the web page. They appear at the very top of your browser window. For example, on the next page you can see the home page of the jewellery retailer Astley Clarke. The title can be seen at the top 'Designer Jewellery | Astley Clarke.com | Over 50 international jewellery designers with next day delivery' (the part at the end '– Mozilla Firefox' is written in by the browser).

Google is extremely interested in what you have titled the page. Google is so interested, in fact, that it presents it as the main link to the page in its search results, as you can see below, where the first result is indeed 'Designer Jewellery | Astley Clarke.com | Over 50 international ...', with Google truncating the full title'.

Because titles are so important, you must devote your full attention to making them as informative as possible both to Google and to the human recipient of Google's search results.

Top Tips for Tip-Top Titles

A title is a summary of a page. Words should be chosen carefully – the title is the first thing people see when they search, so make sure it promises good things behind the blue, bold text of the search result. Here are a few things to bear in mind when writing titles.

- Every page should have its own unique title. Don't repeat the same one again and again.
- Titles apply to a page, not a site, so they should describe the content of the page, not the whole site. If you must reference the site (for branding reasons, say), then do so at the end of the title.
- Word order is important, so 'front-load'. Put the words that are the most important – the most relevant to that page – at the beginning of the title.
- Write a sentence, not a list of words. Remember, you are trying to attract human beings to click on this.
- Only the first 66 characters of a title are shown in Google's search results. You can of course go beyond that, but be aware that Google will cut it short. And if Google's users can't see it, Google is much less interested in it – it may pay a little attention to what's in the title after those first 66 characters, but not nearly so much. Characters include spaces and punctuation.

For reference, a sixty-six character long title looks like this...

- Google knows there may be a difference between Pole[1] and pole[2], and between Sue and sue, and that the capitalised version of each would be equally likely to apply to both meanings. So You Might As Well Write Your Titles Like This. There are a number of

---

[1] He was a Pole, Walter.
[2] He was a pole vaulter.

schools of thought about whether to capitalise words such as 'of', 'to' and 'and', but the rules can get confusing, so if in doubt, Write Every Word In The Title With Capital Letters At The Start Of Each Word.

Directions for Developing Dynamite Descriptions

The title is not the only piece of metadata that is shown in Google's search results. Have another look at the Astley Clarke result:

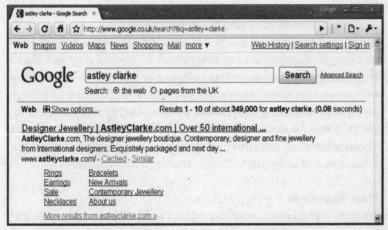

Below the title, in black, sits a snippet of text (truncated to around 160 characters) describing what is on the page: 'Astley Clarke.com, The designer jewellery boutique. Contemporary, designer and fine jewellery from International designers. Exquisitely packaged and next day …'

This metadata is your chance to describe to a searcher exactly what they might find if they click on the link to your page. So it is called the meta description and it is marked up as follows:

```
<meta name="description" content="Astley Clarke.com, The designer jewellery boutique. Contemporary, designer and fine jewellery from International designers. Exquisitely packaged and next day delivery." >
```

Your meta description will not always appear in Google's search results; it depends on what has been searched for. The meta description tends to be used as the snippet if the search terms typed into Google all appear in the title of the page in the results, or if a search is limited to a particular site (using the 'site'[1] operator). For searches for words that include ones that appear in the main page content, but not in the title, the snippet is usually created from the page content that includes these words, with the words themselves emboldened, because Google believes that will be the most helpful to users[2].

Google doesn't care what's in that description – it's strictly for humans, a temptation to click. That click, however, *is* important to Google. Google is very interested in results that get clicks, suggesting that the page was relevant to the search – assuming, of course, that the clicker doesn't come straight back to Google and click something else in the results. And Google is checking for that too. So don't try to trick people into clicking. Be honest about what they will find and only people who are interested in what you are offering will click through to your page.

Meta Keywords

In the bad old days, search engines paid attention to what web pages said were the most important words – the key words – in the page. Unfortunately, this resulted in unscrupulous web page authors trying to trick the search engines.

```
<meta name="keywords" content="spam, spam spam, spam spam spam, spam spam, lovely spam, wonderful spam" />
```

---

[1] A search for 'doctor who site:bbc.co.uk' will only return pages relevant to 'doctor' and 'who' held on the bbc.co.uk website.

[2] Occasionally, Google returns snippets about a page from those written by the volunteer editors of the Open Directory Project (or ODP, found at http://dmoz.org). If you want to stop this happening, place the following line in the <head> of your page: <meta name="robots" content="noodp" />.

Google ignores this metadata completely, as do most other modern search engines.

Language

Google is pretty good at identifying the language of a page without help, but it does no harm to be explicit. Language can be specified using a two-letter code such as 'en' for English, 'fr' for French, 'de' for German and so on. You can also use a two-part code, where the first part specifies a language and the second a geographic variant. The two parts together are called a 'locale'. By convention, the second part is written in capital letters. For example, fr-FR is French as spoken in France, fr-CA is French as spoken in Canada[1].

We can tell Google about the language of a page, or any part of a page by specifying a 'lang' attribute. So, if we wanted to show that all of the text in the HTML of a page was in English, and in particular, British English, we could add a lang attribute to the opening <html> tag as follows: <html lang="en-GB">.

To show that within that page, a quote was actually in French, or at least an attempt at French, we could add the lang attribute to the appropriate <q> or <blockquote> element: <q lang="fr"> ceci n'est pas une pipe</q>. Most tags will take a lang attribute, including divisions, paragraphs, lists, list items, emphasised and strongly emphasised text.

5.1.5 Telling Google about Collections of Pages

Grouping with Navigation

You can use your site's navigation and the resulting directory paths to group pages on your site. This will be done fairly

---

[1] Dialect is not sufficient to define script, and languages where multiple script options are available (e.g. Chinese, Uzbek, Serbian) have script defined as in the following example: zh-Hans_TW implying Chinese in a simplified Han orthography in Taiwanese dialect.

naturally – neatly grouping content is simply what site navigation does, but it is worth noting that Google is paying attention as much as your users are.

The careful use of cross-cutting navigation, particularly on large sites, can reinforce the collective power of a group of pages, turning them into cross-cutting themes. An example of this is the way in which blogs, in addition to their main categorisations, also tag their articles with a number of labels. Clicking on a label brings back a list of all pages tagged with the label. An article may be listed in several tag groups at once.

On-site Search Results

On-site search results are another form of cross-cutting navigation. One of the richest sources of site-specific vocabulary is the input data from a site's own search engine[1]. Every site running a search function should capture and analyse the expressions searched for; feed this into your search demand research process as described earlier.

When visitors to your website use your on-site search, make sure the search results pages that are generated produce a URL in the address bar that features the search terms used[2]. Such pages are naturally full of terms relevant to the search undertaken – including links to other relevant pages in the site – and can be used as 'virtual' content pages. As 'content' pages full of vocabulary relevant to the search terms – along with their unique URL – they can be linked to from within the site as if they were real pages. Here is an example of how this may be useful. Consider a site that sells different sizes of widgets; the

---

1 How well your site performs for searches made on it depends on the sophistication of the search technology deployed, and may not actually reflect the presence or absence of appropriate content on a site, so consider using Google's own search technology (see Google Mini Search Appliance: http://www.google.com/enterprise/search/mini.html).

[2] Use 'GET' as the query submission method, just like Google (www.google.com/search?q=get+post).

site is organised by size, which means all the small widgets are listed on the small widgets pages and all the large widgets on the large widgets pages. A 'blue widgets' on-site search will produce a results page from all the size pages that has only links to 'blue widgets' on it. On its own, this is of no relevance to Google, but the minute you link into this search result page from another location on the site (which is now possible because of its unique URL) as if it were a real content page, you will create a highly optimised page of 'blue widgets' for Google to find and index. Previously your site didn't have such a thing, so now you can be relevant to 'blue widget' searches in a way you weren't before.

Search results as content pages have URLs that will also allow the bookmarking, emailing, and inbound linking of search result pages, which will improve the Reputation of your site.

Google News

You can flag some pages to Google as being news pages – ephemeral, topical, time-sensitive stories that you wish Google News to pick up. A content article intended for publishing in Google's News Search needs to be published at a URL that contains a unique number consisting of at least three digits[1].

Google SiteMaps

Google SiteMaps are specially constructed files that tell Google more about the pages of your site, and the relationships between them. A SiteMap can show Google how often different pages change, to reduce unnecessary crawling; it can also show the date each page was last modified, and the relative importance of different pages on your site to one another.

---

[1] See http://www.google.com/support/news_pub/bin/answer.py?answer=68323& topic=11665 for more details. There is a world of additional detail surrounding Google News love, but we have decided that it is too specialist to cover in any detail in this edition.

If a page has a particular relevance to a location, such as a property on an estate agency website, or a venue on a hotel-listing site, locational information[1] can also be included in the SiteMap.

To find out more about Google SiteMaps, how to produce them and how to register them with Google, see http://www.google.com/support/webmasters/bin/answer.py?answer=40318.

5.1.6 Telling Google about Whole Sites

Whole sites, as far as Google is concerned, are domains. A domain has a good technical description, but in simple terms it's the part of the web address with the dots in, but without the slashes. Some examples of different domains are:

- www.amazon.com
- www.amazon.co.uk
- www.bobspetfish.co.uk

Google sees amazon.com and amazon.co.uk as different sites (although with some strong linking relationships between them).

Location

The most important thing you can tell Google about a whole site is its geographic relevance. Google is providing increasing localisation of results, involving understanding the location of the searcher, the locational intent of the searcher, and the locational relevance of any sites from which search results might be returned. Marissa Mayer (VP, Search Products & User Experience at Google), noted in her blog in 2008:

---

[1] This would be included in either KML, KMZ or GeoRSS format. See http://www.google.com/support/webmasters/bin/answer.py?answer=94554 for more details.

Your location is one potentially useful facet of personalized information. Looking at my questions, the answers to a number of them (What time does J.C. Penney open? How much power does that hydroelectric dam generate? What time does Tropic Thunder play?) require the search engine to know that I was in Yankton, South Dakota and Crofton, Nebraska when I asked. Since location is relevant to a lot of searches, incorporating user location and context will be pivotal in increasing the relevance and ease of search in the future.[1]

A May 2007 patent suggests some of the ways in which Google intends to implement this, detailing a method that geographically targets a search based on the text submitted by the person searching, a location currently being displayed on a map, or the location of the searcher detected via GPS. The patent application also notes some possible page navigation methods, with stored query histories, visual hints of which direction on the map has more results for a query, and a 'click-to-dial' functionality for phone users.

The beginnings of this localisation of search can already be seen with increasing integration between Google Search and Google Maps. Entering into Google Search a generic term such as 'hotels', which typically appears in search queries with a geographic component, now returns a 'local results' search box as the first result on the page.

Localisation can also be seen in AdWords, both in the control panels which allow increasingly sophisticated geographic targeting of ads, and on the front end with integration of Google maps with AdWord copy:

---

[1] M. Mayer, 'The future of search', The Official Google Blog, http://googleblog. blogspot.com/2008/09/future-of-search.html

Quality **Hotel** Heathrow
www.lastminute.com   Quality **Hotel** near Heathrow relaxed and refined ambience.
⊞Show map of London Road, Slough, London, SL3 8QB

Holiday Inn London-Ealing
www.HolidayInn.com   Lowest Rates Guaranteed. Book on the Official Website.
⊞Show map of Western Avenue Hanger Lane, London, W5 1HG

Google's region, city, defined area and point radius AdWords targeting[1] show how sophisticated Google's locality calculations have become. This is not only of interest for targeting desktop ads, but will clearly be critical for mobile ads as technologies improve.

Already, where search queries do include a locality, such as 'London hotel', a map accompanied by a set of local business results for that locality is now frequently appearing at the beginning of the first page of results. The specific references alongside each map are, however, dependent on the phrasing of the search. For example, a search for 'London hotel' produces the following:

Local business results for **hotel** near **London**

A search for 'London Hotels', however, produces a slightly different list:

---

[1] https://adwords.google.com/select/targeting.html

These local map results are consistent – rerunning the query does not result in different results (unlike AdWords, for example).

Country and Language Searches

Google users are offered the option to restrict their searches to pages from the country (and, in many cases, the language) of their regional Google, by selecting a radio button on the main search page. For example, Google.co.uk offers the options to search 'the web' or 'pages from the UK'. Google.fr offers the options 'Web', 'Pages francophones' or 'Pages : France'.

The numbers of visitors making these types of restricted search is comparatively small, but significant. The overall use of the 'pages from the UK' option on Google.co.uk appears to be around 13% of all searches[1].

Google Trusts the Person Doing the Searching

Google pays attention to what people doing searches declare about their own location. For example, a searcher who claims to be in a locale of en-GB (English, UK) will receive the same

---

[1] Hitwise data for April 2008, http://weblogs.hitwise.com/robin-goad/2008/04/how_popular_is_googles_pages_from__the_uk_search_option.html

results when searching from a computer in the UK as when searching from a computer in the USA or from a computer in France. If someone declares that they are in a locale of en-US (English, USA), they will get a different set of results.

French geographic variants, unexpectedly, return the same results as their 'parent' language. A user with a French-Canadian locale gets the same results searching on Google.co.uk as a user with a French-French locale. We would expect Google to get better at differentiating these over time, however.

Where in the World Is Your Site?

Google may trust the person doing the searching, but it's not always so trusting of site owners. It has several clues it can use to determine the location of a website.

- **The top level domain** is the last letters after the dot. So www.google.co.uk has a top level domain of 'uk'. A country code top level domain (ccTLD[1]) such as .uk, .fr, .us, .ca shows where the owner of the domain intends it to be related to. If the top level domain is not country-specific, such as .com or .org, the country can still be declared to Google via Google Webmaster Tools[2] which can sometimes appear in the Google results alongside the URL[3].
- **The language in which a page is written** gives a strong indicator of location – one which may override other cues. Of course, pages written in English may be from the UK, USA, Australia, New Zealand, South Africa and more.
- **The vocabulary on the page** (e.g. 'Paris') may also

---

[1] http://en.wikipedia.org/wiki/Country_code_top-level_domain
[2] http://www.google.com/webmaster/tools
[3] http://googlewebmastercentral.blogspot.com/2009/12/region-tags-in-google-search
    -results.html

give locational clues on some sites – vocabulary within titles, headings and link text are valuable pointers to relevance to a location, as are contact postal addresses.

- **The registered location of a server** (its IP Address) can be mapped to a country. Google has been explicit that it uses this as part of its determination of location.

- **The postal addresses registered against a domain name** may also provide a hint. If a company owning a domain is based in Ireland, then the site held at that domain is probably relevant to Ireland to some degree.

- **Google Maps/Google Local Business Centre registration** explicitly ties a website to a geographic point. To register, go to www.google.co.uk/local/add/.

- **The patterns of external links** to a site from other sites can be used to determine relevance to a location. This element appears to be an important way in which Google currently understands location. This is unsurprising, as the patterns of linking sites are likely to be more 'correct' or 'wise' when demonstrating the regional relevance a site may have.

The growing importance of geographic relevance to Google searches, together with the authority and trust that comes with being a real organisation in a real place, means declaring a locational relevance is becoming a necessity, not an option. However, the question of how to do it without then potentially compromising your site in the results that Google has decided are location-independent (i.e. from the default 'Web' search as opposed to the 'Pages from' option) does not yet have an answer.

5.1.7 Telling Google Nothing, and How to Avoid It

Deep, Dark, Hidden and Invisible are all names given to those parts of the web that, to date, have not been accessible to bots, and so have not been indexed. There is also a grey area of content which, while indexed, has rendered itself obscure or of low value to Google in some way.

Orphaned pages are perhaps the most common example of obscured content. An orphaned page is one that is not linked to from any pages on its own site, only from a page (or pages) elsewhere on the web. As far as Google is concerned, if it's not important enough for you to show it to all visitors to your site, it probably isn't important enough to rank well. A review of your server logs to find pages that have never been requested may well bring up a list of potential orphans.

Technologies such as PDF documents and Flash can also push content into the shadows, as they do not provide the kind of detailed structural markup around text that HTML does. Scripting technologies such as JavaScript and methods such as Ajax can call up new content in response to a user action (as can Flash), but unless very carefully implemented, much of this may be rendered totally invisible to Googlebot.

Content held behind forms can also be unavailable to Googlebot – this is of particular concern to Google, as there's a lot of juicy information out there in databases that is currently masked by the need to fill in fields and press buttons before you can get at it. However, the good folks at Google are working on allowing Googlebot to fill in simple forms to see what is behind them. But why make it difficult?

Video and audio content provided through Flash, Quicktime, MP3 and similar technologies are also a problem for Google, and if you intend to offer these technologies – and the content in them is useful – then ensure that any content presented within such rich media formats is also available as plain text[1].

---

[1] YouTube now offers automatic transcription via its captioning service (see http://googleblog.blogspot.com/2009/11/automatic-captions-in-youtube.html).

Video is worthwhile content. Google's search results often include still-image references to relevant video content it finds, providing it comes from approved video partners, such as Google's own YouTube and Google Video websites, and increasingly from reputable third-party sites such as Metacafe[1]. Such video stills in the search results pages make for a very compelling result for a user to click on, and can only be achieved by submitting your video content to one of these sources. These visitors will not be arriving on your site, as the result will take them to the likes of YouTube, but your video content will be far more accessible to searchers in this form and therefore ultimately more likely to result in a visit, particularly if your website URL appears conspicuously in the video itself.

Do You Have a Problem?

Implementing interaction-rich or mixed-media websites is a process fraught with risk of blocking or confusing Googlebot, and if you're intending to create one, it's probably time to get the professionals in. However some simple questions can help you decide if there is likely to be a problem:

- Is there text in there somewhere?
- If you turn off JavaScript, can you still get to all the content you want Google to see?
- If you turn off Flash, can you still get to all the content you want Google to see?
- If you need to use PDFs, are the contents described in detail on a HTML page that links to the PDF?
- When clicking, hovering or otherwise interacting with a page, does new content appear without the URL changing?

If the answer to any of these questions is 'No', then you may have a problem. If the content to be indexed is available only

---

[1] http://www.youtube.com; http://video.google.com; http://www.metacafe.com

through the application interface, Google will not find it. It therefore becomes essential to provide some sort of site map – in clearly marked-up HTML – that provides a path into the data for Google to find and crawl.

Perhaps the worst problems stem from situations where non-HTML technologies are used to provide navigation functions for a site, links to content that cannot be actioned from outside those media; if this is the case you may find that large numbers of links to locations across your site are invisible to Google.

Case Study

A major national estate agency firm asked us if their website could perform better in Google. They had provided a set of links available to Googlebot to provide sets of properties at different locations. However, Google was indexing only a tiny proportion of their available properties. We determined that the property listings at any location were paginated into sets of ten. To move to the next page of properties, the user had to click on '2' for page 2, '3' for page 3 and so on. These links to the subsequent pages were implemented in JavaScript only. Without JavaScript, only the first ten properties were available to Googlebot to index. Mystery solved.

5.2 MANAGING REPUTATION FLOW

There is a stream of technical management that is separate from the structuring Visibility work detailed in the previous section, but which is essential in the process of building a site for Google. This stream of work involves managing the flow of Reputation a site has acquired to ensure it is attributed to the places it can most positively appeal to Google.

5.2.1 Love's Boundary Is Your Domain

The boundaries of human love are usually pretty clear, to human beings. When loving people – as opposed to football teams or chocolate – the object of someone's love is defined by the biological boundaries of (usually) a single other human organism. Men don't mistakenly love the sisters of their wives the same way they love their wives just because they are from the same family; each man knows where his wife begins and ends.

Google's love has boundaries too, and while Google loves many, many websites at the same time – not being subject to human conventions – the boundaries of its love for each of them is defined by the registered domain name[1] at which the site operates, such as bobspetfish.co.uk. A registered domain name is the human-readable permanent name that we recognise as the main web address of a website, which is then associated with the Google-readable (and potentially temporary) numerical address that has been assigned to the specific computer on the internet that hosts the technical files and programs that make up the site. These permanent names look like bobspetfish.co.uk – names that can be clearly identified and remembered by people – while the numerical addresses look like 66.102.9.104, which are unambiguous technical locations at which the information can be found.

For the purposes of this book, it is not necessary for you to know how the internet puts these names and addresses together, you just need to know that it does. Google knows that the domain names are more useful to its searchers than the numerical addresses, because they are more usable and memorable, and also because they are less likely to change than the numerical details. Consequently Google presents domain names in its results as the targets of its ranked results for searches.

---

[1] http://en.wikipedia.org/wiki/Domain_name

You may have noticed that we didn't say that Google's boundaries are defined by the registered domain names, in the plural, under which the website operates – which in Bob's case could easily include bobspetkoi.co.uk and bobsgoldfishbowls. co.uk if Bob wasn't aware of Google's love being unique for each domain it finds. Google may work out that a group of domains used by one organisation are in fact related to the same operation, but as with our family example at the beginning of this section, Google's passionate love for one of them does not mean a passionate love for all. When Google evaluates the Relevance and authority of these individual domains it confines itself to the Reputation associated with each in isolation and ignores the rest.

The best practice for a website courting Google's love is therefore to operate from as few domain names as possible. The fewer there are, and this means predominantly one if possible, the more concentrated the site's Reputation will be and the better regard Google will have for it. This means:

- bobspetfish.co.uk, bobspetfish.co.uk/koi, bobspetfish.co.uk/goldfishbowls are GOOD;
- bobspetfish.co.uk, bobspetkoi.co.uk and bobsgoldfishbowls.co.uk are BAD.

5.2.2 Reputation Flow Internationally

Google recommends that if you run websites that are targeted at different regions of the world, particularly if they are in different languages, then you should consider operating from regional domain names that reflect the country you are targeting. In Bob's case this would mean bobspetfish.es if he wanted to start selling to people living in Spain and bobspetfish.cn if China was his target. But hang on a minute: separate domains dilute Reputation and force Google's love to be spread across multiple websites reducing performance in natural search as a consequence; don't they? Er, yes, they do. So what is Google up to, recommending something that is at odds with an utterly core principle of how its assessments of Reputation work? Boy, we wish there was an easy answer to this one. At the time of writing, there is no subject that preoccupies us more on behalf of the websites we work with than solving the conundrum of fewer or more domains and effectiveness in international search markets.

The simple truth of the matter is that Google's recommendation to dilute across multiple international domains is based on two assumptions:

1. That you will carefully manage the flow of your Reputation across and into your multiple domains, so that the sum of its parts is equal to the whole and not less.
2. That your operations in international markets will necessarily develop their own local reputation – i.e. links from other websites within the territory in question to your regional domain – which will help Google decide if they are actually useful to inhabitants of that country or not.

On the face of it, a carefully managed programme of regional domains, where the love each receives is carefully shared with its peers in other regions, if relevant – for example, at a product-to-product page level – would appear to be the most effective scenario. However, in our experience, these assumptions are simplistic and rarely reflect the realities of running an online operation that is trying hard to be effective across multiple international territories. And this apparently simple solution is almost never either simple or actually a solution.

One of the main reasons that country-level domains are not simple is that it is frequently impossible to acquire the equivalent domains to your first domain in every region you want to operate in. Very few organisations looking to be more effective online in international markets have the advantages of an Amazon Inc., who had the foresight and now has the clout to secure pretty much any 'amazon.' domain it desires. In Bob's example, it turns out that there really is a Bob Spetfish who lives in Spain and registered the bobspetfish.es domain from which to promote his eponymous dental practice[1]. And besides, the Spanish are highly unlikely to use 'pet fish' as a search term when looking for goldfish to buy, so his carefully researched trading and domain names would look a bit ridiculous to a Spanish speaker, particularly if there are any unfortunate combination in that string of letters that may suggest something inappropriate[2].

Before suggesting any sort of method for you to evaluate your options and to approach this problem for your organisation, we need to throw another spanner in the works.

5.2.3 Google Loathes a Clone; Abhors a Duplicate

This is a big, complex section. If you have a smallish, simple site, it is unlikely that the issues around duplication will be particularly troublesome; however, that doesn't excuse you from persevering with the pages of SEO fundamentals that follow. This part of the book addresses a critical problem for many websites, and has some challenging solutions to propose.

In the pursuit of real usefulness Google removes from its results all but one item of information that it considers to be essentially the same as others it has found. The notion behind this approach is that presenting more than one copy of the same thing to a user does not constitute 'usefulness', so they don't it. Google chooses the information with the best Reputation – relevant to a specific search – to keep in its results and all the others disappear. The information isn't removed from its index, it is simply filtered from the results of that search. This happens

---

1 No, not really, we made this one up too.
2 For example, 'pet' in French means 'fart'.

at a level across domains and within domains; we'll come to the latter in the next section – it is the 'across domains' consideration that is relevant to the use of multiple international domain names.

To extend our 'Google love' analogy to cover duplicates: Google is rather good at spotting a pale imitation of the object of its affection. Clones that look identical but are lacking the integrity of a lovable personality don't fool Google, nor is it fooled by someone else in the mask of its beloved.

A duplication example from Bob's goldfish site may include the moment when, being a bit lazy and unethical one day, he copied a whole article on how to choose food for koi from the website of Britain's best-selling[1] koi magazine – www.koimag.co.uk – and placed it on his site. A few days later, Google visited Bob's website and indexed the new article – well, new to his site, anyway. Google's duplication-checking process spotted shortly afterwards that this was essentially the same as the article on the koi magazine website, and in the course of assessing the relative Reputations of these two URLs, Google decided that koimag.co.uk had more Reputation. The results of subsequent searches on Google by users interested in how best to feed their koi do not contain both koimag.co.uk and bobspetfish.co.uk, because Bob's URL has been filtered out.

Bob's example may not reflect the behaviour of your organisation regarding the appropriation of other people's information, but the impact may be the same. Consider a scenario where, following Google's recommendation, Bob decides to set up bobspetfish.com to reach the US market. He will use all of the English-language content from his UK site at bobspetfish.co.uk, altering the British spellings to American spellings, because this is a tiny proportion of the words on the site and will take little effort to change, but may make a positive difference to his US customers. Shortly after the new website

---

1 Allegedly. We've not verified this claim.

goes live, Google finds it and indexes all his information. Imagine Bob's disappointment when he cannot find his new site on either Google.com or Google.co.uk, using search expressions for any of the information in it – he keeps just finding the UK site. Google has decided that all the pages on the new site are effectively the same as the pages on the UK site – despite the fact that they are not identical – and, because the UK site has been online for longer, it has acquired greater Reputation, so is preferred.

Bob's scenario happens all the time for many organisations that present essentially the same information in the same language – English being the worst offender – on multiple international domains, targeting their individual markets. Google subsequently prefers the domain or URL with the best Reputation regardless of the location of the searcher, the Google site on which they are searching, and what really would be most useful to them. This is a flaw in the otherwise effective use of Reputation by Google, and one we expect it to resolve in the fullness of time. Until then, each organisation must minimise the duplication of information across its domains as best it can in order to improve the chances of searchers finding the most appropriate version for them. Because every website and every organisation's online objectives are different, there cannot be one set of recommendations that will work for everyone trying to avoid the filtering of legitimately targeted information from Google's results pages. For now, we can offer an approach to help you identify if your information is likely to trip a duplicated content filter, and a set of ideas that may help you work around these limitations of Google.

When Is a Duplicate the Same and When Is It Different?

Google's definition[1] of duplicate content goes like this:

---

[1] http://googlewebmastercentral.blogspot.com/2006/12/deftly-dealing-with-duplicate-content.html

- It has to be a substantive block.
- It has to completely match (i.e. be identical) or be appreciably similar.

Google says the following aren't considered duplicate:

- Translated content from one language to another.
- Smaller chunks and snippets that can appear on more than one page.
- Oh, and everything that doesn't meet its duplicate definition![1]

Sadly, this isn't very helpful, because it is so vague. So how do we really know whether content is going to be filtered out or not? Well, we encourage you to look at it from a common sense point-of-view. The main body content of a URL of information, particularly if it is structured properly for Google to understand, is going to be the substantive content on the page, so if this appears anywhere else where it is also the main body content, it is going to get filtered. If you attempt to fool Google into forgetting that the content is effectively the same by making small changes to the copy, you will probably fail. Common sense tells us that if the content isn't rewritten to some meaningful extent, Google is probably going to spot its similarity and filter it out. So, if you are unable to stop similar content appearing on different domains of yours (assuming you can't rationalise your operations onto fewer domains in the first place) then you must make an effort to rewrite any content that runs the risk of tripping Google's filters.

The ultimate purpose of minimising duplication is to manage the flow of the Reputation you acquire into as few locations as possible, so they become truly authoritative and relevant in Google's eyes. Multiple domains with multiple copies of content

---

[1] Actually, it was Steve who said that one. In frustration.

are a level of dilution almost beyond hope. But we must hold off looking further into these conundrums because there is another issue to tackle first.

Holding Still the Moving Target of Google's Love

The duplication of precious web information is not the exclusive territory of organisations ill-advisedly operating from international or multiple domains and of unscrupulous copiers, such as Bob, on a bad day. Duplication happens all the time within a domain and at the bidding, albeit often unintentionally, of the site owners themselves.

Duplication can be simple. Imagine that Bob has written what is possibly the most informative, clear, enjoyable and downright poetic article on the care of goldfish ever written. Calling it 'Goldfish Care' not 'Care of Goldfish' to more consistent with the way users look for this type of information, he puts it in three categories on his website – 'care', along with 'care of tanks and bowls'; 'goldfish', along with 'goldfish varieties'; and 'articles', where he holds all his articles in one place regardless of topic. It therefore ends up at three separate URLs:

www.bobspetfish.co.uk/care/goldfish-care

www.bobspetfish.co.uk/goldfish/goldfish-care/

www.bobspetfish.co.uk/articles/goldfish-care

Bob then decides that it is such a great article, he'd like to draw some attention to it by paying for some advertising on the *Practical Fishkeeping* website and through Google's sponsored search results[1]. Being a web marketer of growing confidence he remembers that he should be tracking whether or not visitors actually come from either of these sources using his web analytics system. He decides that the best way to do this is to

---

[1] See http://AdWords.google.com for further information.

create a new URL for each of the sources he is inviting the visits from, so that he can look at the analytics 'content' report[1] to see how many people come from each advert. These new URLs look like this:

www.bobspetfish.co.uk/articles/goldfish-care?FishkeepingMag Advert

www.bobspetfish.co.uk/articles/goldfish-care?GoogleAdWords

These URLs both present exactly the same page, because Bob's web server ignores the characters after the '?', but the fact that they exist is still recorded in Bob's web analytics system.

This stuff is simple, self-inflicted duplication which, unintentionally, has created five URLs at which visitors can experience Bob's inspiring content, and five potential targets to which they might link to provide the site with a fillip of cracking Reputation. This is not a good thing for Bob's site, because the Reputation that the information acquires may easily be split across these five locations, diluting it in the process. And if you think that sounds bad enough, there are other, more subtle, and equally unintentional types of duplication to be aware of.

Imagine that Bob locates his brilliant article at www.bobs petfish.co.uk/articles/goldfish-care/. People love it. They link to it – again and again. But people are, well, a bit slapdash. After a few months, there are a few variations of that article URL:

- Fred cuts and pastes the address from his browser address bar into his list of favourite carp links on his website. He misses off the trailing '/':
  http://www.bobspetfish.co.uk/articles/goldfish-care

---

[1] At this point, if you are unfamiliar with these concepts, you may want to jump forward and have a quick look at chapter 6 Using Google to Grow: Better Lovin'.

- Wilma references it in her fish-blog. She misses off the 'www.' on the front:
  http://bobspetfish.co.uk/articles/goldfish-care/

- Barney finds it via the site's internal search engine. Weird address, but hey. He posts it in a goldfish forum:
  http://www.bobspetfish.co.uk/index.asp?page_id=58 28595304

- Betty types it into her review article. She gets the domain wrong, putting '.com' instead of '.co.uk':
  http://www.bobspetfish.com/articles/goldfish-care

- Bambam types it into his MySpace page. He sees that it doesn't have a filename at the end of it and adds the most likely one. It works, so he posts it:
  http://www.bobspetfish.com/articles/goldfish-care/index.html

Now Bob has registered the .com version of his domain too, just in case he decides to chase after the US market, as we discussed earlier in this chapter. But in the meantime, he has set his web server to catch variations such as the missing slash and the missing www to avoid the visitor getting no page at all. Unfortunately, the server simply serves an identical page at each of these locations, forming five more duplicates of the same page. Google finds all of these variants of the article's location when it crawls the sites on which the links appear and applies the Reputation it finds at each source link only to the specific URL referenced, diluting the potential Reputation the article could enjoy a further five ways. The consequence is that the article fails to enjoy the rankings it deserves.

Google's Active Duplication Management

Google knows content duplication is a problem and is attempting to solve it in three main ways:

1. Telling website owners a bit about how it works and then telling them to do things differently to help avoid the problems that arise (see the 'deftly-dealing-with-duplicate-content' footnote on p. 162 and keep reading for the bits we believe are actually useful).
2. Automatically attempting to glue together the Reputation it finds across duplicate URLs within a site and point it all at the most likely real target.
3. Providing a technical option for site owners to specify which URL is the preferred one for situations where duplication could cause a problem.

Google's communication to website owners includes the information about how to specify which URL is the one that all the Reputation should be focused on[1]. This allows website owners who are otherwise unable to make their sites work properly for Google to supplement the information they provide in the metadata with something called a 'canonical' tag. Anything in its canonical form is the thing reduced to its simplest and most significant form, which in URL-speak means the URL you want all the Reputation focused on. In Bob's case, he has decided to follow Google's advice and identify www.bobspetfish.co.uk/goldfish/goldfish-care/ as the canonical location for his brilliant article. He does this by placing the following tag in the <head> of the HTML for this page:

```
<link rel="canonical" href="http://www.bobspetfish.co.uk/goldfish/goldfish-care/" />
```

---

[1] http://googlewebmastercentral.blogspot.com/2009/02/specify-your-canonical.html

This means that whenever this page is visited by Google at any of the possible duplicating URLs on Bob's site, it will be entirely clear which one Bob wants all the Reputation focused on. Consistent use of this tag is intended to supplement the information Google discovers about how people are choosing to link to Bob's content to help it make better decisions. And use of this tag[1] would clearly be advisable for your site, if you are unable to prevent the duplications themselves.

Before Google invented the canonical tag it was trying to do this all by itself, and in an article[2] explaining one of the ways it deals with duplications, the author stated the following:

> *How we help users and webmasters with duplicate content*
> We've designed algorithms to help prevent duplicate content from negatively affecting webmasters and the user experience.
>
> 1. When we detect duplicate content, such as through variations caused by URL parameters, we group the duplicate URLs into one cluster.
> 2. We select what we think is the 'best' URL to represent the cluster in search results.
> 3. We then consolidate properties of the URLs in the cluster, such as link popularity[3], to the representative URL.
>
> Consolidating properties from duplicates into one representative URL often provides users with more accurate search results.

---

[1] With your own data in it, naturally – no use telling Google that your canonical URL is on Bob's site.

[2] http://googlewebmastercentral.blogspot.com/2007/09/google-duplicate-content-caused-by-url.html

[3] Link popularity is Reputation.

While the ideas promoted by Google to manage the content duplication you may have already caused are doubtless effective, they are nowhere near as effective as not duplicating the content in the first place. Nowhere near!

The reason for the title of this section is that we believe the most effective way to manage the risk of content duplication is not to let Google experience it at all. The beauty is that doing so is relatively simple, requiring only a few rules that can identify all possible duplication situations and a bunch of settings on the web server that holds your website.

It is now time for us to introduce you to a great ally of Reputation flow and the Swiss Army knife of duplication-avoidance: the permanent redirect[1].

The permanent redirect – also known by its HTTP standard[2] status code number, 301 – is a simple method by which a request for a particular URL[3] is met with a notice that refers whoever or whatever is asking to another URL where content will be permanently found. The 'whoever' could be any user visiting with their web browser, and the 'whatever' could be Google rolling up with Googlebot to index the site.

One URL to Rule Them All

Permanent redirects set up on Bob's server will therefore intercept all the references to the duplicate versions of the URL for his goldfish care article, with all their mistakes and misspellings and weird strings of numbers, and permanently redirect them to his canonical URL, www.bobspetfish.co.uk/goldfish/goldfish-care/. This elegant solution will most likely be completely lost on the human visitors to Bob's site – paying

---

[1] Plenty of further reading can be found at: http://en.wikipedia.org/wiki/URL_redirection – compare 301 with 302 and 307, which are frequently used in error, when a 301 would have been better.

[2] http://www.w3.org/Protocols/rfc2616/rfc2616.html

[3] This is a technical request to the web server, not someone phoning Bob asking him for the page.

more attention to the information than the intricacies of the URL they are actually on – but it will be a revelation to Google. All roads lead to one single URL for each unique page of information, which means Google has only one place to channel any Reputation it may have found for each of them – despite the mistakes that the other sites may have introduced into their links – and no post-rationalisation exercise is necessary to attempt to amalgamate the Reputation it has found.

Unfortunately Bob learned about the permanent redirect months after he had launched his site, and he was concerned about all the URLs Google already had in its index for the duplicates. He needn't have worried, because ultimately Google came looking for the information it found at the duplicated URLs by requesting them again, at which time it discovered the permanent redirect and dropped the old URL like a stone, passing any residual Reputation the old duplicated URL may have acquired onto the canonical URL.

Alongside this redirection exercise Bob stopped his own unintentional duplicating – where he created copies by allowing the URL to reflect the way the visitor got to the article, namely via 'care' or 'goldfish' or 'articles'. He did this by linking to the article from URLs within these sections and not by creating a new URL when the page was visited. So wherever in the site a visitor came from, when they clicked on a link to the article it was to the canonical form of the URL that he had chosen. But again he was worried about the versions of this page Google had already indexed at the other URLs and what would happen to any Reputation they may have acquired. The permanent redirect came to the rescue again by referring any requests for the old URLs to the canonical form, which was a redirection largely intended for Google. Along came Google in due course to check that the information at the old URLs was still there; it then experienced the redirect and dropped the old URL and applied any Reputation to the canonical form as before.

One of Bob's last tasks in making sure his URLs are as hygienic as they can be is to look at those he created for the advertising links: www.bobspetfish.co.uk/goldfish/goldfish-care?FishkeepingMagAdvert and www.bobspetfish.co.uk/gold fish/goldfish-care?GoogleAdWords. If he redirects these, he will lose the ability to track the visits, using his free web analytics tool from Google[1]. Bob can't see how he can both track these URLs and redirect them to avoid duplication, so he decides to simply rely on the canonical tag for these visits, hoping that few people will use these URLs if they end up linking to the article and that Google will successfully amalgamate the Reputation if they should. This is an adequate compromise for a website on the scale of Bob's but it wouldn't be for a more enterprise-level organisation. With a little more technical ability and knowledge it becomes possible to allow the server to accept the request for the advertising URLs and, before redirecting them, capture the data about the source of the visit, so that both objectives are achieved: one URL to focus Reputation and a successful analysis of the source of the visitors.

5.2.4 The Unavoidable Change of Heart; a New URL to Love

There can be many legitimate causes for the object of Google's love to change. The organisation behind a website may have decided to move domain names – out of opportunity or necessity – or to improve the technologies behind the site itself, which causes a review and an opportunity to optimise URL structures. These are a few of the possible reasons, but the impact is the same: new domains[2] and URLs that are new to Google are new domains and URLs that have no Reputation.

---

[1] http://www.google.com/analytics

[2] WARNING: It is possible that the new domain under consideration has had a previous life. Do your due diligence properly to ensure its historical reputation is not likely to harm it. Try MajesticSEO.com and Archive.org for your research.

Unless you take great care to migrate your site's existing Reputation to these new domains and URLs, so that it flows seamlessly from one to the other, it will be like starting your site all over again, with a frequently catastrophic effect on your natural search performance.

> The only difference between improving Google's love for an existing site and a new site is how you manage the flow of existing Reputation from a previous website domain or a set of previous locations to their new optimised form. Everything else is the same. Existing sites have Reputation that is associated with specific domains and URLs and needs protecting and migrating. Please don't leave it behind if you have to move.

Changes just to URLs within a domain can be taken care of simply by a comprehensive migration plan that captures all requests for the old URLs and utilises permanent redirects to induce Google to pass the existing Reputation on to the new URL. If you are lucky, there will be enough information in the old URL alone to identify the new URL – perhaps one of those pesky article ids that are unique to a single page of content – and a simple rule can be written to compose the necessary target of the redirect. When there isn't enough information in the old URL you have a number of options about how to progress:

1. Audit your existing site for all its URLs and create a mapping file where the old URL is the subject of a look-up to find the new URL at which to point the redirect. This sounds easy enough, but can be somewhat intimidating for a large legacy site, where often no-one actually knows what all the old URLs are or could be, or where to find them.
2. Create a plan for the URLs on your site that you think are important and migrate just those. This assumes that you

will cover all those that really are important, and in our experience it only works on relatively small sites; on bigger ones, too much falls through the cracks.

3. Use your web analytics system to identify all the landing pages that are the start point of a visit to your site and migrate just those with permanent redirects. This assumes that all the links that pass Reputation to your site also deliver visits, which in our experience is not a reliable assumption.

4. Look at the data from your registered Google Webmaster Tools and Majestic-SEO[1] accounts where extensive lists of the links that exist to your site will be found, along with all the target URLs. Create a migration plan that just includes these URLs. This assumes that there are no other significant, Reputation-passing links out there. This is getting closer to an acceptable scenario, in terms of its resilience.

5. A combination of the above usually works best.

When implementing permanent redirects it is very important that Google experiences only a single redirect. It is not okay to first permanently redirect Google from, for example, http://bobspetfish.co.uk/index.asp?page_id=5828595304 to http:// www.bobspetfish.co.uk/index.asp?page_id=5828595304 (note the absence and then inclusion of 'www') and then apply a second permanent redirect to http://www.bobspetfish.co.uk/ goldfish/goldfish-care/ because this will seriously risk losing the Reputation you are trying to protect, in the process. The correct permanent redirect must be from http://bobspetfish.co.uk/ index.asp?page_id=5828595304 to http://www.bobspetfish.co. uk/goldfish/goldfish-care/ without the intermediary step. This can increase the complexity of your server redirection rules, but not by that much.

---

[1] Visit http://www.majesticseo.com for more information.

Such migrations from one set of URLs to another within a domain can have surprisingly little negative impact on visits referred from Google's natural search, despite the wholesale change to the objects of Google's love. However when migrating across domains the impact can be more noticeable.

The principles and methods for migrating Reputation across domains are identical to those within domains; the URLs just happen to include a change to the domain element. The impact on search performance is different because there is an unavoidable period of time during which the Reputation the old domain and its URLs had acquired is split between the old domain and the new domain – a period of time that is dependent on the pace at which Google revisits the old URLs and therefore experiences the redirection. Google's appetite for your site is not a mystery – go and look at your Google Webmaster Tools account where the crawl statistics[1] are recorded – but the pace of its crawling your old URLs is very dependent on the Reputation you already have. Sadly, for some sites this can mean that URLs deep in the site may not be crawled more often than monthly, so that your Reputation may not recover for a couple of months. During this sort of migration, both URLs will be receiving requests as a result of existing links from around the web and search results for URLs that haven't been migrated yet. As a consequence, particularly of the former, I'd advise you to leave your permanent redirections in place indefinitely.

5.2.5 Love Yourself with Internal Links

In human life, love is rarely forthcoming for those who have a difficult relationship with themselves. The truism that one must love oneself before expecting anyone else to do so, seems to be,

---

[1] Log into your Google Webmaster Tools account and visit https://www.google.com/webmasters/tools/crawlstats to see these.

well, true. It is true for Google's love too. Whether the love you show for your own website takes the form of careful structuring of information or painstaking research into market demand, it all contributes to Google's love for the site. There is, however, a particular issue that has a special place in this chapter regarding the flow of Reputation within your own site.

As a website gets larger and more extensive – as its content grows – Google pays more and more attention to the patterns of linking within the site itself in order to assess the relative Reputation of the many pages of similar (but not duplicated) content it may find. Yes, I'm referring to the Reputation that a site generates for its own pages, by the patterns of links that exist within its own domain. These internal patterns of Reputation supplement the external patterns of Reputation Google has found in the rest of the web, to help it choose a single relevant page from a site to represent in its results when there are many that would be suitable. This is an important part of Google's assessment of the most useful page of a site for a searcher to see, particularly if few of the internal URLs of a big site enjoy direct links from the outside.

For Bob's growing site, we begin to see that a number of pages are acquiring more and more internal Reputation because of the simple fact that they are linked to on every page. These pages are the top sections of his site – for example, the 'goldfish bowls' section and the 'goldfish care' section – and appear in the main navigation for the site on every page. As a consequence, in a simple way, these pages are acquiring more of the Reputation that the site has to share across its pages, and Google will see it. These patterns of internal links are one of the primary drivers for the population of Google's Sitelinks[1]. Sitelinks are a set of links that Google presents below the result for a site to URLs within the site in order to make the result even more useful to

---

[1] http://www.google.com/support/webmasters/bin/answer.py?answer=47334&topic=8523

searchers. Sitelinks only appear for websites that Google believes to be authoritative for the search term entered.

BBC - Homepage
Breaking news, sport, TV, radio and a whole lot more. The **BBC** informs, educates and entertains - wherever you are, whatever your age.
www.**bbc**.co.uk/ - Cached - Similar - 💬 ⬆ ✖

Football	Africa
Sport	CBeebies
iPlayer	Radio
News	On TV

More results from bbc.co.uk »

Illustration 3: The BBC website in Google's results for a search 'BBC', showing Sitelinks

We wouldn't be surprised if a simple analysis of all the links on the BBC's website showed that the eight URLs in Illustration 3 had the most Reputation internally, irrespective of their external Reputation. That said, Google is using external Reputation as another of the primary drivers for the population of these links. The final driver for the choice of these links is 'search refinement', which in simple terms means that if Google finds that a significant proportion of searches for the BBC also include the word 'football', such as 'bbc football news', then it will include the page with the best football Relevance and authority on the BBC site in the Sitelinks list. This is a simple example that hopefully demonstrates part of Google's approach to Sitelinks, which reinforces the importance of the linking patterns within your site.

Bob decides that because he wants to see if there is a real growth in demand for shubunkin goldfish he is going to increase the internal Reputation of the variety page for the shubunkin he has for sale by linking to it from every page that mentions any goldfish varieties, along with a promotional link on the home page. Sure enough, the next time Google updates the Sitelinks for Bob's site there is a link directly to his shubunkin page. Result!

With regard to your site, the challenge of managing internal Reputation grows with its scale. The bigger your site, the more links there are to manage, but also the more internal Reputation you can muster for the important URLs. There is no escaping the job of carefully auditing the link patterns in your site, and deciding how best to manage them in the interests of the pages you really want to be winning the search races. Make sure that you don't have a splatter-gun approach to linking within your site; in other words, rationalise the links that exist on each page into two types: those that link back up the hierarchy of information to the home page, and those that link to content directly related to the current page. Avoid having masses of links to pretty much all pages, on all pages. This produces an almost impenetrable noise of links for Google and the Reputation of key areas of your site will suffer as a consequence.

5.2.6 Anchor Text; the 'Love Letters' of Reputation Flow

Cast your mind back to chapter 2 How Does Google Work? and in particular to section 2.6 Assessing the Authority of Content. In this section we explained the disproportionate importance of anchor text, where the anchor refers to the text that is associated with a link in its HTML construction. A link is constructed of two main components, the target URL and the text that represents the link on the source web page. This text is frequently simply the URL itself, such as www.bobspetfish.co.uk/goldfish/goldfish-care/, but can also be a carefully chosen piece of relevant content that the owner of the source site has deemed fit to qualify the link. In Bob's case, people are starting to link to his article with words like 'the best info on caring for your goldfish' and 'neat goldfish care article'. Because of the importance Google applies to these words – in its assessment of their democratic vote for Bob's article – they are magic for Bob's Reputation. However, there are a bunch of people who simply use Bob's URL for the link, which then puts www.bobspetfish.co.uk/goldfish/goldfish-care/ in the anchor text, and because the word 'goldfish' and the phrase 'goldfish care' are in there anyway, it's a winner too. But let's just reflect a moment on Bob's site in a parallel universe, where Bob2 has not been reading *50 Ways to Make Google Love Your Website* and has URLs for his website that look like this:

www.goldfishemporiumltd.com/files.php/?contentid=344992

Bob2 has also written a great article on caring for goldfish, but at least half of the external links that the site has acquired don't use any special anchor text, just the URL. Sadly, the otherwise powerful additive of relevant vocabulary to the Reputation of Bob2's article is missing, so it doesn't rank highly in Google's results when searchers look for information on caring for goldfish. Influencing the choice of anchor text by sites that link to your information is notoriously difficult, which is why vocabulary-rich URLs are so important.

Internal Anchor Text; Love Letters to Yourself

Anchor text is as critical to the successful loving of your own site as it is to how others express themselves. It is therefore essential to consider carefully how you apply anchor text to the links within your site, so as to make the most of the relationship between the information on the source pages and the information on the target pages, and help Google with its assessment of Relevance. One of the really smart ways to do this is to map the vocabulary from the findings of your user demand analysis (see chapter 3 Create Your Website for Your Users) onto the categories and sections of your website, and actually apply them as the anchor text on your internal links. Yes, we do mean to encourage you to let the user demand data inform your information architecture process, because this has two profound benefits for your site: widespread Relevance to your target market for Google to assess, and reassuringly familiar vocabulary all over your site for users to explore.

Avoid expressions such as 'click here' or 'more ...', and where possible, present links as a complete phrase within a normal sentence – this can complement another shorter link to the same target within navigational menu parts of the page. Ideally, the main heading of the target page should be referenced in the anchor text of the link.

Bob takes this advice on board for the specific issue of his goldfish care article and makes sure that from the 'care' section of his website he is linking to his article using 'feeding and caring for goldfish' and from his 'goldfish' section he is linking using 'caring for goldfish and fancy goldfish'. On the home page he simply uses the general form 'caring for goldfish'. The difference is subtle but it makes the anchor text more relevant to the source page of the link, thereby enhancing its potential to increase the Relevance of the article page to a wider range of searches.

5.2.7 Location Naming in Reputation Flow; Hey, URL, Got a Name?[1]

In the previous sections we have talked about the power of the anchor text in influencing Google's perception of the Relevance of the page of information at the other end of the link. How that anchor text is constructed is therefore of great importance, and while you have little editorial control over the linker, you can make sure that using the URL itself will come close to being ideal, by filling it with vocabulary relevant to the information. Naming your URLs to reflect the Relevance of the content found on them is therefore an essential process in making Google love your site.

You may have been unaware of how much control it is possible to have over the construction of your own URLs.

---

[1] This pun only works if you pronounce URL as 'url', one word, rather than reading out each letter.

Changing the content of your URL can be easy or difficult, depending on the software or technology you use to run your site, but it is rarely impossible, and more and more software is now available with URL-naming built in[1]. Changing URLs to reflect the content of the information is a key optimisation technique because of its influence on the anchor text of the links that it may subsequently enjoy. The vocabulary chosen to go in the URL has a small positive effect on Google's perception of the Relevance of the information on the page anyway, but its main potential comes from its power as anchor text.

Naming your URLs therefore involves applying the findings you gained about the demand that exists in your market – chapter 3 again – to the information contained both on the pages of your site and in the URLs that represent them.

Bob refers to the user demand analysis he undertook and decides that the general URL for the home page of all his information and subsections about the different types of goldfish will be www.bobspetfish.co.uk/goldfish/ while the home page for all the information about shubunkin will be www.bobspetfish.co.uk/goldfish/shubunkin/. The latter differs from the URL he started with, which was www.bobspetfish.co.uk/shubunkin/ but he doesn't worry about that, he just configures a permanent (301) redirect from the /shubunkin/ URL to the /goldfish/shubunkin/ URL and all is well.

Clearly Bob's been paying attention to the importance of Reputation flow, and although his site has only been live for a few months, he diligently sets up his redirects to take care of any small Reputation these sections may have already acquired. If you change your URLs for naming and anchor text reasons, you too must take care to redirect any existing Reputation to the new URLs.

---

[1] Also look into mod_rewrite for the Apache web server (http://httpd.apache.org/docs/1.3/mod/mod_rewrite.html) and the Isapi Rewrite engine for Microsoft's IIS web server (www.isapirewrite.com).

One of the web's leading retailers is Amazon Inc., and they have long understood the importance of Reputation flow, but not much of how they manage it is visible to mere huma www.amazon.co.uk/Ways-Make-Google-Love-Website/dp/1905211252. This information is automatically generated from the product name – with a bit of automatic culling of words that it doesn't think are likely to be relevant (in this case, '50', 'to' and 'your') – and a unique product identifier – which in this case is the international standard book number for this book. Any link to this URL is therefore going to have some very relevant vocabulary in it, which will help Amazon's page be more relevant to anyone trying to make Google love their website.

When doing a Google search for '50 ways to Google love'[1] Amazon's UK page for the book is in second place behind our own website, and there is the handsome and relevant best-practice URL for all to see.

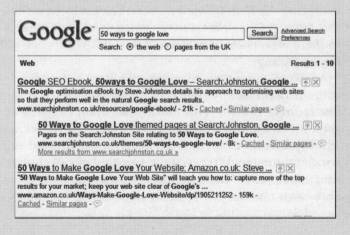

---

[1] No, you're right, not many people who don't already know this book exists will try this particular search, but that's not the point we're trying to make.

Now that we've made our point, you may think we can move back to the main text, but we can't. Amazon applies a level of Reputation flow management that is really quite sophisticated and pretty much invisible to the human visitor, and it is worth describing it here. This URL also works: www.amazon.co.uk/exec/obidos /ASIN/1905211252, as does any version which includes an Amazon affiliate code[1] such as www.amazon.co.uk /exec/obidos/ASIN/1905211252/johnstocouk-21 which visitors experience in their browser, and can use to link to. That last type is particularly prone to linking by Amazon's millions of affiliates, because it earns the affiliate (identified by the last part of the URL[2]) a few pennies if you buy the products after having visited the URL. You may wonder, therefore, if Amazon has sacrificed its concerns about duplicated content and Reputation flow in favour of facilitating the affiliate market. Well, it hasn't: Amazon has a very clever way of managing the Reputation flow when Google looks at the site, because Googlebot is never going to buy a product, so there is no point in protecting the affiliate id when it comes visiting.

Amazon's approach to managing Reputation flow, without permanently redirecting human visitors, is to just redirect Google. This means that when Googlebot asks for www.amazon.co.uk/exec/obidos/ASIN/19052 11252/johnstocouk-21 it is permanently redirected to www.amazon.co.uk/Ways-Make-Google-Love-Website/ dp/1905211252 where all the Reputation from the affiliates is also allowed to collect. Amazon knows when Googlebot is visiting because Google makes that very

---

[1] https://affiliate-program.amazon.co.uk/
[2] Er, Steve in this case.

clear by declaring that it is Googlebot in its User Agent[1]. This is proving to be a very effective strategy for Amazon to maintain that one URL to rule them all, in the one place it really matters – Google's index – without compromising its users' needs of the site.

Big URLs Don't Try[2]

When naming your URLs there are some other considerations to bear in mind. You should make sure that the URL of each page is relatively short, is readable by a human, and makes sense when looked at in isolation. For example, www.bobspetfish.co.uk/goldfish/goldfish-care/ tells us a lot about what we can expect at this location, which means it passes this human-readable test. Being human-readable is a good defence against mistakes being made in the use of your URLs as links, as well as an element of website best practice that is good for other reasons[3]. This applies both to the filenames you choose and the directories they are held in. So, for example, we recommend using hyphens for spaces – they read well, they are prettier than underscores when underlined (compare <u>this-version</u> and <u>this_version</u>), and we know that Google accepts them as word dividers.

An example of quite a good URL:

www.bobspetfish.co.uk/goldfish/fancy-goldfish/oranda-goldfish/

An example of a really bad URL:

www.bobspetfish.co.uk/lib/cont/type43/query?pageid=3456789x87&ccid=3456

---

[1] A User Agent is a text string that is usually sent in the http header field *User-Agent* to identify the application.

[2] With apologies to Frankie Valli and the Four Seasons.

[3] See http://www.useit.com/alertbox/990321.html – yes, that really was written in 1999.

It's not bad because Google can't read it or store it in its index; on the contrary, Google is pretty tolerant of all sorts of nonsense in your URLs. It's bad because it undermines both the likely accuracy and the Relevance of links, which is, frankly, an unforgivable combination.

5.2.8 Pulling Together the Strands of International Reputation.

Way back in section 5.2.3 Google Loathes a Clone; Abhors a Duplicate, we promised to return to the conundrum caused by the challenges of managing multiple international domains – as Google recommends – while attempting to avoid the pitfalls of content duplication. Well, we're going to keep our promise, but at a relatively shallow level, because we have yet to make the same recommendation twice when working with such web operations, due to the specifics of each situation, and we don't want to generalise if it really won't be helpful.

The sections you've read since we made this promise will have filled in a lot of the picture for you of how Google interprets the flow of Reputation that exists between sites and the main issues that affect it. And from the work we have done on the websites of international businesses, we have learned that despite Google's enthusiasm for localisation its sensitivity to the actual location of the web operation in its results, and the actual location of the searcher, is relatively poor. This means that if your site is in English, it will not be excluded from any Google[1] aimed at an English-language market – UK, USA, Canada, Australia, South Africa, etc. – until a user requests only 'pages from the UK' or the equivalent, but even then Google isn't infallible. And in French, Google doesn't

---

[1] Google runs a ccTLD for most countries on the planet: http://www.google.com/language_tools?hl=en (scroll down).

seem to mind if the site is in France or Canada as long as it is in French.

The consequence of Google's lack of real sensitivity (for now) is that if forced to give a general recommendation about what to do about this conundrum, and if you are starting from scratch, we'd err on the side of 'one URL to rule them all' for each language, on a single domain – such as a .com – so that all Reputation for each page of information in each language ends up in one solitary location. We believe this is easier to manage than multiple copies of same-language content across multiple locations – even within the same domain – just lying around waiting for Google to deduplicate them, and easier to move on from when the situation changes, which it doubtless will. From there we'd recommend a subtle change in the content on each language page based on where the visitor is coming from; for example, change the currency to US dollars if you have identified (from the user's IP address[1]) that the visitor is in the USA, or to sterling if the user is in the UK. Googlebot typically comes from the USA, so either let it be a US visitor or strip out the currency information when it comes along. Keep any changes between what Google sees and what a visitor sees to an absolute minimum, as Google has been tricked before by sites that attempt to artificially influence the flow of visitors by showing Google one thing and users another[2], and it takes a very dim view of such practices.

There, we've made a recommendation, phew. We hope it shows we have thought about solving these problems in some detail, but that it doesn't provide you with enough rope to hang yourself. Solutions to these problems – if they exist at all – are profoundly sensitive to the specifics of each situation, and a

---

[1] There is software and data you can plug into your web server that will capture this data and make it available to your web site software.

[2] Called 'cloaking' by the SEO community (see http://en.wikipedia.org/wiki/Cloaking).

general book like this cannot hope to address them all. But take heart, there is usually a compromise to be wrung out of your predicament, sufficient to bring you a fresh gush of Google's love and its consequential free visits.

This concludes the process chapters of the book, where we have been explaining how to build Relevance, Reputation and Visibility into your Tripod of Love, so that Google finds your site completely irresistible. We will now look at how to move on from this good start, by understanding how your site is performing and what steps you should take to keep a cycle of continuous improvement working.

50 WAYS . . .

25. When putting the technical building blocks of your website together apply Web Standards. Google loves Web Standards.

26. Valid and fast-loading HTML is a quality signal to Google, so be vigilant to what's in the source code, even if you've never looked there before. *See section 5.1*

27. Emphasise the phrases and sentences that are important on your website, by the careful use of italics and emboldening. *See section 5.1.1*

28. Present headed paragraphs with effective semantic mark-up using heading and paragraph tags. And nest headings at different levels to identify the structure of longer pieces of content. *See section 5.1.2*

29. Order items in your page that are lists of phrases, words or even sentences, in list tags. Include your navigation items as lists. *See section 5.1.2*

30. Only use blockquote and table tags for quotes and tabular data respectively, not for layout. *See section 5.1.2*

31. Divide the page content into relevant chunks or blocks by using division tags. This helps segregate the important from the unimportant content. *See section 5.1.3*

32. Spend five minutes crafting a better title tag for a page. Title tags are remarkably important because they also feature as the link in Google's results pages. *See section 5.1.4*

33. Increase the click-through rate of your pages when they appear in Google's results by writing highly complementary and compelling descriptions to accompany your titles. *See section 5.1.4*

34. Group your pages by using internal links so that they reflect the patterns of Relevance on your site. *See section 5.1.5*

35. Use your own search result pages to group unlinked-to but otherwise relevant content from across your website. *See section 5.1.5*

36. Use a Google SiteMap feed to tell Google automatically where all your URLs can be found and which are the most important. *See section 5.1.5*

37. Tell Google where your business is based, through the Google Local Business Centre and/or the geo-targeting option in Google Webmaster Tools. *See section 5.1.6*

38. Avoid hiding rich content in proprietary applications, such as PDFs, Flash, etc. and in databases that cannot be queried by Google. By all means use them, but allow Google-friendly versions, such as video transcripts. *See section 5.1.7*

39. Minimise the number of web domains from which you operate, because Google loves each on its own merits and Reputation can be diluted if you have more than one. *See section 5.2.1*

40. Target international markets only after composing a balanced view that combines your existing Reputation, your ability to acquire country-level domains and your appetite for local Reputation-development. There is no one way to acquire Google's international love, and this is one of the most complex issues you'll have to deal with. *See section 5.2.2*

41. At all costs avoid the duplication of content at multiple URLs across your site(s). And if you *really* can't avoid it, manage it through the use of the canonical tag. Think of each piece of content having a 'home' URL that all roads must lead to. *See section 5.2.3*

42. When you move content from one URL to another, tell Google by configuring a permanent redirect from the old URL to the new one. *See section 5.2.4*

43. Organise and manage the patterns of your internal links, so that your Reputation flows to the important URLs (this may be the same as or different from Way 34, depending on your site's needs). *See section 5.2.5*

44. Organise and carefully select the words chosen for your internal links. Remember anchor text is immensely powerful, even within your own site. *See section 5.2.6*

45. Create URLs that describe the content that is found at them. Relevant vocabulary in a URL translates to perfect anchor text when others use it in links. *See section 5.2.7*

6

USING GOOGLE TO GROW: BETTER LOVIN'

You have structured your web pages, written the copy and put it all out there ready for visitors and engaged with your marketplace. Well done. You have reached the end of the beginning. You have now constructed something – your website – with which you can identify clear opportunities for improvement and measure the effects of all the actions you take from here on. For the sake of argument, assume that your site is getting about one tenth of the love it deserves from Google. Your task is to identify the improvements – simple and obvious at first, more subtle as you continue – that will deliver the rest.

You may feel that this 'one tenth of the way to love' cannot possibly apply to you, especially if you are already an established business. But a target is not necessarily for reaching, it is for aiming at. As the poet[1] said: Try again. Fail again. Fail better.

6.1 GOOGLE ANALYTICS

For Google to love your site fully, your visitors must love your site too. Your visitors will tell you how they might love you better, if you watch carefully, and analyse how they use your site. Is a process confusing? Is an article interesting? How are people moving through the site? When is the best time to tell them about things you want them to know about in addition to the information they have come to find? The process of

---

[1] Samuel Beckett: http://en.wikiquote.org/wiki/Samuel_Beckett

analysing their behaviours to find answers to these questions and more is known as website analytics.

Google wants its love for you to achieve its full potential, so it gives you the key to its heart – a powerful free analytics package, unsurprisingly named Google Analytics.

Google can justify giving such a powerful tool away because it gives Google an insight into how people behave on sites that it could not obtain in any other way. This in turn means that it can better understand the relative values of different links on a page by considering which ones receive more use by real humans. There are many other analytics tools on the market, some free, some costing many thousands of pounds. We know of no free analytics tool that beats the power of Google's, and we would suggest that you don't even consider paying money for something more sophisticated until you find that you are no longer gaining valuable insights from Google Analytics. This may take years.

Setting up your site on Google Analytics is straightforward, requiring a short script to be inserted on every page. Go to www.google.co.uk/analytics and register and verify your site.

6.1.1 Measuring Google Love with Google Analytics

To successfully measure Google's love, you must first be able to distinguish natural search from other traffic. Google does this for you quite neatly in Analytics.

Example

Bob successfully sets up Google Analytics on www.bobs petfish.co.uk and logs in. From the menu on the left of the Google Analytics 'Dashboard', he selects 'Traffic Sources', 'Search Engines'.

Bob is interested in the period 30 March 2009 to 29 April 2009, so he selects this in the resultant page:

Just under the words 'Search sent 6,134 non-paid visits via 9 sources', there is an option to show 'total', 'paid' or 'non-paid' – Bob is always careful to choose 'non-paid' to ensure that he is only seeing natural search results. He makes sure he does this on every page he visits.

Bob sees from the table at the bottom that Google is responsible for the bulk of visits into the site. From the 'Views' icons he selects the one that looks like a pie chart to see the percentage. Google turns out to be responsible for 90% of all natural search visits, a fairly typical result for a UK site. Bob clicks on the word 'google' in the table to examine just the visits from Google itself.

Google Analytics returns another page showing visits coming from Google from each 'keyword'; in reality, this shows search queries that delivered visits into the site. At the bottom of the list Bob can see a 'Find Keyword' option.

Find Keyword: containing ▾ [   ] [Go]
Go to: [1]   Show rows: [10 ▾]   1 - 10 of 1,547 [◄] [►]

Bob decides to see how the launch of his content initiatives around goldfish care and goldfish diseases in July and early December affected Google's love for his site. He types in 'care' as the keyword to find and clicks 'Go'.

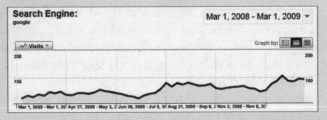

Bob can see that his work has had a positive effect, although the daily figures make the results rather 'spiky'. He chooses to graph by week instead, using the icons at the top right.

Search Engine:
google   Mar 1, 2008 - Mar 1, 2009 ▾

◜ Visits ▾   Graph by: [ ] [ ] [ ]
200   200
100   100

Mar 1, 2008 - Mar 1, 20| Apr 27, 2008 - May 3, 2| Jun 29, 2008 - Jul 5, 2| Aug 31, 2008 - Sep 6, 2| Nov 2, 2008 - Nov 8, 2(

There is now no doubt. The articles paid off with better lovin' from Google.

Two key Google love indicators available from Google Analytics are:

1. **Visitor numbers from generic search phrases.** By generic, we mean searches that do not mention your brand name, so if you work for Acme Chairs Ltd, 'office chairs' would be a generic search and 'Acme office chairs' would not. You cannot help but rank well for your own brand name, so filter it out to ensure you are getting a clear love signal. There are two ways you can do this using Google Analytics: one is by the Advanced Segments capability, which will be the more robust analysis, and the other is by choosing the 'excluding' option in the Find Keyword search described above (while remembering to select 'non-paid') and typing the word 'acme' into the box.

   The Advanced Segments version of this analysis is configured as follows. From the Dashboard, click on 'Advanced Segments' and construct a new segment by taking a copy of the default 'non-paid traffic' segment to get you started. Add an 'and' statement: the 'Keyword' should have the condition 'Does not contain' of 'Acme' (insert your own brand name here). Make sure that 'case sensitive' is not checked. If you have a number of brands to exclude, add some 'or' statements with new 'Does not contain' conditions. The segment will look something like:

Once the segment has been created, you can filter any report to view the figures by generic natural search by using the 'Advanced Segments' options at the top right of each page. Select 'Visitors' and apply your segment to see the figures.

2. **The length of the long tail.** The greater the number of unique phrases you are receiving visitors for, the more Google thinks you are relevant to the demand in your market. You can find out how many unique phrases are delivering visitors in Google Analytics by looking at Traffic Sources > Keywords (and showing the 'non-paid' figures, naturally). The page will report how many non-paid visits were sent via how many keywords. At present, Google Analytics does not offer graphing capabilities for the number of keywords, so you will need to track the number of keywords reported yourself over time. Use this as a warning sign as well as a measure of success – any falling off of numbers may be a sign of serious problems.

We cannot hope to cover all of the intricacies of Google Analytics in this book, it's just too large a subject. We would, however, recommend the following resources for learning more about it:

- www.google.com/support/googleanalytics/ – the basics.

- www.google.com/support/conversionuniversity/ – become a more knowledgeable Google Analytics user.

- analytics.blogspot.com/ – the latest tips and tricks.

6.2 MARKET SHARE AND MARKET VOLUME

Market share and market volume analyses concentrate on identifying patterns where volumes of demand exist that your site is not taking advantage of – where the market volume is high and your market share is low.

This is not something that Google will do for you – you need to obtain data yourself and mine it for insights. This can be done quite simply by matching proportions and trend data from the Google Keyword Tool against the proportions of visits being generated by those same phrases into your site.

The theory is simple – if your site is receiving all the love and therefore all the traffic it could compete for across your subject area then you might expect the proportion of visits to your site for a given set of exact phrases to be the same as the proportion of Google's declared search volumes for those phrases.

If you are seeing some considerable variance in those proportions, this may point to one of the following issues:

- You are ranking, but people aren't clicking. Consider how page title text and meta descriptions might be improved.

- You are not ranking well, but there is the opportunity to do so with some better content. Consider what articles or categories might help performance.
- The figures at your disposal are just statistical flukes. Reduce the chances of this by taking them over fairly long time periods.

Example

Bob decides to perform a short gap analysis by comparing phrases that deliver visits into www.bobspetfish. co.uk with phrases that are searched for on Google. He goes to https://adwords.google.co.uk/select/Keyword ToolExternal and obtains the approximate average search volumes for goldfish tank (and tanks) and goldfish bowl (and bowls).

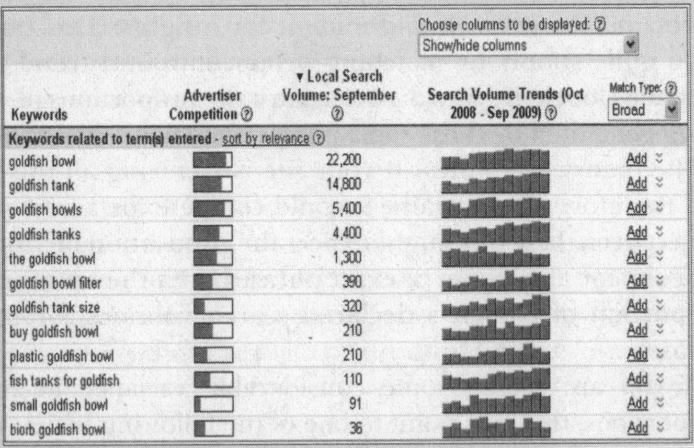

| | | | Choose columns to be displayed: ⑦ | |
| | | | Show/hide columns ▼ | |
Keywords	Advertiser Competition ⑦	▼ Local Search Volume: September ⑦	Search Volume Trends (Oct 2008 - Sep 2009) ⑦	Match Type: ⑦ Broad ▼
Keywords related to term(s) entered - sort by relevance ⑦				
goldfish bowl	▬▬□	22,200		Add �
goldfish tank	▬▬□	14,800		Add ≋
goldfish bowls	▬▬□	5,400		Add ≋
goldfish tanks	▬▬□	4,400		Add ≋
the goldfish bowl	▬▬□	1,300		Add ≋
goldfish bowl filter	▬▬□	390		Add ≋
goldfish tank size	▬□□	320		Add ≋
buy goldfish bowl	▬□□	210		Add ≋
plastic goldfish bowl	▬▬□	210		Add ≋
fish tanks for goldfish	▬□□	110		Add ≋
small goldfish bowl	▬□□	91		Add ≋
biorb goldfish bowl	▬□□	36		Add ≋

Bob then logs into Google Analytics and obtains the average number of visitors arriving at www.bobspet fish.co.uk from the same exact phrases. He compares them to see if the proportions are similar between the demand in the marketplace and the visitors reaching his site.

The proportions are as follows:

	Google Keyword Tool	bobspetfish.co.uk analytics
goldfish bowl | bowls	1	1
goldfish tank | tanks	0.70	0.08

Bob sees that proportionally, there should be more demand for tanks than he is currently delivering on. He adds 'articles on goldfish tanks' to his list of things to do.

6.3 SOPHISTICATED MARKET ANALYSIS

More sophisticated market analyses can be carried out by comparing a long list of search phrases with demand proportions, comparing them all to each other, two at a time, in a large matrix. While this can prove extremely valuable, it is difficult and time-consuming.

Access to Hitwise data (we first mentioned Experian Hitwise way back in section 3.8 Advanced Search Demand Analysis) can also be of great value in accurately determining your website's share of market and size of market on a per-phrase or per-pattern basis. Investigating this thoroughly takes a great deal of expertise, and is probably something best achieved by 'getting a man in'.

6.4 VALUING IMPROVEMENT

In analysing the performance of your site, you may identify that you need to improve the ease of use of the site (usability), or to enable more people to access the site (accessibility), or to target and improve Google natural search performance around particular pockets of demand (search engine optimisation). In order to calculate the likely return on investment in such efforts, you need to be able to assess the likely value of improvements to your site's performance, so we shall start there.

Let's begin with putting a value on the primary aim of your site. For a commercial enterprise this is straightforward – what is the average value of a sale?

Example

Bob knows from his Google Analytics that a typical bobspetfish.co.uk customer makes three purchases of average value £30 each per year: £90 per year in total. Bob makes an average profit of 50% on every product he sells, so he places a value on each new customer of £45.

For a non-commercial site this is more difficult, but some attempt can still be made.

Example

Veg-o-crats is a charity which asks people to grow their own vegetables to reduce food miles and carbon dioxide production[1]. A Veg-o-crats questionnaire suggested that 20% of the people who signed up to a Veg-o-crats email reminder[2] planted some vegetables and would not have done so otherwise. The study also revealed the average size of crop produced, and how much of that was used.

---

[1] No, actually, it isn't, because we made it up. If you wish to start such a charity, please feel free to call it Veg-o-crats, as we haven't registered that domain name, although I suspect someone else might have done by now.

[2] APRIL: plant lettuce!

Veg-o-crats were able to quantify the value of 'growing your own' in terms of carbon dioxide saved, by referring to carbon trading exchange rates. They calculated that the average value to the planet of someone growing their own veg is £10 per person, making the value of signing up for the email reminder 20% × £10 = £2 per year.

These measurable actions – the sale, the email sign-up – are known as 'conversions'. They are the point at which a person converts from being a visitor to a customer. Other typical non-purchase conversions include:

- an email sent;
- a telephone call made[1];
- something downloaded – such as a piece of software or a PDF document;
- a form completed – or even just a part of a form completed;
- a live 'chat' started;
- a comment or a forum post made.

In each of the examples above an attempt should be made to link them to a value measure. For example, if a telephone call is made, what proportion of callers convert to a sale? Where it is extremely difficult to determine, try even a notional value – for example, you may decide to treat a comment in a forum as equivalent to a hundredth of a typical sale – you can always change it later if it seems to be skewing your decisions. Once you know the value of each conversion, two critical questions can be answered.

---

[1] Careful consideration must be given to how best to track these conversions. A distinct phone number might be used so that you can count the number of inbound inquiries the website generates separately from other marketing channels.

- **Question 1: how likely is a visitor to convert?** The average conversion rate can be obtained by taking the total number of conversions, dividing by the total number of visitors, and multiplying by 100 to get a percentage. A typical conversion rate for a retail site selling small items would be in the range 0.5% to 5%, but it can be more for highly targeted sites.

  Conversion rates are affected by usability considerations such as how easy the site is to use and how well signposted its contents are. They are also affected by how well targeted the visitors are. It is this last point – when the visitors are arriving from Google – that we are most interested in.

- **Question 2: what is the average value of a visitor?** The visitor value is the total value of all conversions divided by the total number of visitors. This may be anything from fractions of a penny to many hundreds of pounds, depending on what you are selling and the profitability of a conversion.

We are also particularly interested in dividing up visitors by phrase or demand type, and considering the different conversion rates and average values they exhibit.

Example

Bob only has one real conversion that he wants to track: a sale. The site achieves an average conversion rate of 3%: for every 100 visitors it receives, three will make a purchase, on average. Bob makes a profit of £3,600 on conversions in a typical month, and the site receives 8,000 visitors over the course of that month, so as a rule of thumb he assumes that if he spends less than 10 pence on winning a new customer, then he's comfortably ahead.

However, Bob thinks that some visitors may be more valuable to target than others, so he sets out to determine which.

First, he creates the segment 'all natural search', containing all those visitors arriving from clicking on a result in Google's natural[1] search results. For the time being he is not interested in people who type bobspetfish.co.uk directly into their browser, or people who follow a link to Bob's site from another site, or people who click on his goldfish care article.

He further segments those arriving from natural search into 'goldfish' and 'fancy' segments. The 'goldfish natural search' segment contains those visitors arriving from key phrases containing any of the main patterns goldfish, common, comet and shubunkin. The 'fancy natural search' segment contains those arriving from key phrases containing any of the patterns black moor, bubble eye, butterfly tail, calico, celestial eye, fantail, lionchu, lionhead, oranda, panda moor, pearlscale, pompom, ranchu, ryukin, telescope eye, and veiltail. These are not all of the 'goldfish' and 'fancy' related terms that bring in visitors, but together they account for around 92% of natural search visitors, which Bob feels is good enough.

An examination of the conversion rates for these segments reveals that the goldfish segment was responsible for 63% of all natural search visitors, and had an average conversion rate of 2.4%. The fancy segment was only responsible for 29% of visitors, but had a conversion rate of 6.1%.

---

[1] Google also calls these 'non-paid' or 'organic' search results, depending on the context.

Bob decides that this is worth further investigation, so he checks the value of sales that each segment was responsible for. Bob has already set up his analytics to report on the profit of each sale made, so it is a simple task to determine the value to his business of each segment.

Overall	*Monthly*
Visitors	8,002
Conversions	240
Average conversion rate	3.0%
Profit	£3,600.00
Average profit per conversion	£15.00
Average value of visitor	£0.45
Segment: natural search	
Visitors	6,134
Conversions	210
Average conversion rate	3.4%
Profit	£3,200.00
Average profit per conversion	£15.24
Average value of visitor	£0.52
Segment: natural search: goldfish	
Visitors	3,866
Conversions	93
Average conversion rate	2.4%
Profit	£1,722.00
Average profit per conversion	£18.52
Average value of visitor	£0.45
Segment: natural search: fancy	
Visitors	1,778
Conversions	109
Average conversion rate	6.1%
Profit	£1,332.00
Average profit per conversion	£12.22
Average value of visitor	£0.75

Based on the results of his analysis, Bob decides to spend £6,000 as a one-off investment in producing content aimed at bringing more visitors into the fancy goldfish area. He's mainly costing his own time, but he may bring in a copywriter to help. He knows that if the investment results in 5,000 extra visitors over the course of a year, he may be looking at a very acceptable return of around 75% per annum. This would require little more than a 5% increase in visitor numbers, so Bob is pretty confident.

There is a final piece to this jigsaw, however. Bob is becoming very conscious of how much time it takes to produce the compelling content he wants on his website, and knows that his time must be valued, as there is just one of him. He will watch carefully how this initiative pans out and will then have a better idea of how time spent on these various efforts translates into profits. There are a lot of other variables – seasonal variation or a great editorial link from another site may skew the measurements – but Bob resolves to keep a close eye on the performance of each segment and not make any hasty decisions.

6.5 GETTING THINGS DONE

Measurements are only effective if people see them frequently enough to actually keep them in mind when making business decisions, and if reporting them avoids information overload. There must also be clear targets for increases, and a process to deal with decreases, in each measurement.

Google Analytics makes reporting easy. You can schedule it to email custom reports to several email addresses, as a PDF document for ease of reading and printing, or as a CSV file for further processing in a spreadsheet.

Here are some tips for spreadsheet reports:

- Use visual aids. Use green for good and red for bad (because up and down, increase and decrease can be either, depending on the measure). Give up-trends up ▲ arrows and down-trends down ▼ arrows. Again, this is a visual aid to understanding.

- We are poor at relating to pure numbers, but we're good at comparisons, so show a comparison over time, such as a percentage change.

- How good? How bad? When is it very bad? Set thresholds and show warnings when they are crossed. Warning thresholds are likely to be different for different indicators.

- Set targets for improvement and report against those targets.

- Show who owns the indicator – who needs to fix any problems or be congratulated for any successes.

- Ideally, phrase your indicators in such a way that any increase is good and any decrease is bad. This makes it a lot easier to assess.

Measure	This Week	Last Week	Change	Target	% of Target	Warnings	Owner
Average cost per conversion	£110	£90	▼ 22%	£100	110%	Off target	Bob Spetfish
Average cost per visitor	£60	£40	▼ 50%	£40	150%	Problem!	Bob Spetfish
Average revenue per visitor	£212	£200	▲ 6%	£210	101%	-	Bob Spetfish

Illustration 4: Example Analytics presentation – green/red would be used to show good or bad.

Great reporting is pointless, of course, unless there is a process in place to make sure that it results in appropriate action.

1. Identify all possible stakeholders – who will this information help to do their job better?
2. Agree two or three measures per report per person, and agree a frequency of reporting. Different people with different responsibilities will need different measures:
   - someone with overall strategic responsibility may need to see visitor numbers from generic search and visitor conversion rate on a monthly basis;
   - a manager might need to see visitors divided into new versus returning to assess the effect of marketing efforts on a weekly basis;
   - someone with implementation responsibilities might need to see visitor numbers and rate of conversion per key phrase on a daily basis when testing page improvements.
3. For every measure a person receives, ask what actions they would take if it increased by 10%, and what actions they would take if it decreased by 10%. If they can't answer the question, they may not need the measure reporting to them. If they do know the answer (or you do), you could even write this into the report. Actions may be:
   - Identify problem measures and target them for further analysis. Do you need a usability test? A questionnaire? A deeper investigation of the analytics?
   - Identify the likely problems influencing the measure. Have you made any changes recently? Any changes from competitors?
   - Pilot a fix for the problem and measure the effect.
   - If it works, roll out the fix. If it doesn't, try different fix, or investigate further.
4. Set targets for improvement. Even if you don't meet your targets, by setting them you ensure that people keep the measures under consideration. If you want to take it to the next level, consider setting high (but reasonable)

expectations for improvement, and pay bonuses based on successful attainment of those goals.

5. Agree regular meetings to discuss the data and review measures. For most people, this type of data is new and unfamiliar; because of this, you'll need to take time to constantly revisit the indicators and their use until they become institutional knowledge.

6. Identify within your process the points at which it's time to get help in. Sometimes, things can get just too difficult, and every organisation will have a point at which it's simply not worth developing the internal expertise to deal with a problem. It's time to get someone in who spends their entire professional life eating and breathing the subject. When to bring in the professionals can be a thorny issue, which we attempt to address in Appendix 1: Should You Get Help In?.

6.6 GOOGLE WEBMASTER CENTRAL AND GOOGLE WEBMASTER TOOLS

Google Analytics is not the only tool that Google provides to measure its love. Google goes to enormous lengths to keep owners of sites informed about its guidelines and best practice. And if there is one resource you should be paying attention to on a daily basis in your pursuit of Google's love, it is Google Webmaster Central at http://www.google.co.uk/webmasters/. Google even has a whole area devoted to SEO advice[1] and has published its own SEO guide[2]. So it is our fundamental recommendation that you should read *everything* Google tells you about the configuration and management of websites within its Webmaster Central area. It is time extremely well spent.

---

[1] http://www.google.com/support/webmasters/bin/answer.py?hl=en&answer= 35291

[2] http://www.google.com/webmasters/docs/search-engine-optimization-starter- guide.pdf

The Google Webmaster Tools (GWT) area is a slightly different beast from the Webmaster Central area in that it gives advice specific to your website. Once you have authenticated yourself with Google as the owner of your site, GWT alerts you to obstacles to love that you may otherwise never be aware of. Google wants to love your site, so takes great pains to inform you of these obstacles in detail. Google will tell you about a number of things, which you should check on a regular basis (even daily), including:

- Errors and problems encountered by Google's crawlers while accessing pages on your site, such as pages that are unreachable, or that fail to load fully, or that simply don't exist (Diagnostics > Crawl Errors).
- Potential problems with page titles and meta description information (Diagnostics > HTML Suggestions) – are they too long, too short, or duplicated?
- Which search queries are returning your site. It also tells you which of them were clicked (Your site on the web > Top search queries). If you are returning terms that are never clicked, it may be time to work on those page titles and meta descriptions.
- Which pages on your site have links pointing to them from other sites (Your site on the web > Links to your site).
- Which phrases appear in the anchor text of links into your site from elsewhere (Your site on the web > Links to your site > Anchor text).
- How many pages on your site are crawled by Googlebot per day, how many kilobytes it is downloading of a typical page, and how long it spends downloading a page[1] (Diagnostics > Crawl stats).

---

[1] From this we can see that the size of the page, and how much of it is tasty text compared to wasted structure, is an important issue for Google.

- Whether Google is considering adding sitelinks to
  your search results. Sitelinks are additional links
  Google sometimes generates from your site contents
  in order to help users navigate your site, and are
  returned for certain queries (Site configuration >
  Sitelinks).

Google will also let you tell it some things:

- Your geographic location (Site configuration >
  Settings), if you don't already imply it through a
  country-specific domain name.
- Whether you want to include images from your site
  in its image labelling program (Site configuration >
  Settings).
- How often you would like Googlebot to crawl your
  site (Site configuration > Settings).
- How you want Google to handle any URL para-
  meters, such as those appended for tracking
  advertising (Site configuration > Settings)
- URLs that you want removed from Google's index
  (Site configuration > Crawler access > Remove URL).
- If you are about to move your site to a new domain,
  and what that domain is (Site configuration >
  Change of address).
- Where your Sitemaps feed is located (Site
  configuration > Sitemaps).

And if you want Google to love your site and you aren't
paying attention to what it is telling you on a daily basis, then
don't blame us when it is clearly falling out of love, but you
aren't listening. Make GWT your home page and pop in every
single day, without fail.

50 WAYS . . .

46. Use web analytics tools, such as Google Analytics, to measure the natural search visits you get from Google that do not include the name or brand of your business. These are generic visits and they demonstrate best how your Google love is growing. *See section 6.1*

47. Measure the length of the tail in the natural search visits of your analytics before and after you make changes. An increase in the numbers of different search expressions delivering visits are a simple indication of how you are doing. *See section 6.1.1*

48. Become a fanatical follower of everything Google publishes for Webmasters by visiting Google Webmaster Central every week, and check the reports for your domain in Google Webmaster Tools every day. *See section 6.6*

49. When Google appears to have fallen out of love with your site, don't panic! Carefully analyse the recent changes you have made and if there is insufficient cause within them, sit tight and be patient. It usually turns out to be a passing mood.

50. The principles of Google's love are unlikely to change significantly in the future. So, if in doubt about how to proceed, remember the Tripod of love and ask yourself, 'What would Google do?'

AFTERWORD: THE FUTURE OF GOOGLE

Google is developing all the time. Applications such as Analytics, AdWords and Checkout appear to be helping to define the web economy; Google mobile and its Android operating system are helping to move computing onto people's phones. Search itself grows ever more sophisticated, while developments such as social networks and cloud computing provide a bewildering array of new concepts to absorb, and new information and relationships for Google to index and serve back to us.

When first writing this book we attempted to produce a set of predictions about what we imagined Google would be doing in the near and medium term future, and how that might affect how you should run your website. However, we found it very difficult to keep up with Google's patents, announcements and developments at the same time. The predictions either came true before we could finalise the copy – such as Google Goggles – or began to seem less likely to achieve what Google had perhaps hoped for them – such as Orkut. So, while we have opinions we are happy to share with you[1], we decided that for the book, we would instead focus on the future of Google that you are probably most concerned with: tomorrow.

WILL GOOGLE BE DIFFERENT IN THE MORNING?

You may have read a bit about Google's search engine and, if

---

[1] From time to time, we'll publish a few of them here: http//www.search johnston.co.uk/googlelove/future.

you have, you have probably come across stories in which innocent websites are suddenly rejected by Google and most of the search traffic referred their way disappears. This has happened in the past when Google has made widespread (but subtle) changes to the way it assesses Relevance and authority, and it is very unfortunate for the sites concerned, but it is rare and unpredictable, so there is no point worrying about it. Google is working all the time to improve the quality of its results in the face of more and more aggressive attempts by spammers to manipulate its results. The very nature and scale of this battle means there is occasional collateral damage. Again, no-one can predict where and when, so you simply have to make sure you are doing the best you can to be true to Google's preferences for the way owners operate their sites[1] and read every detail of the things it tells you about SEO[2].

So while there is definitely a chance that Google will be different in the morning, it is also definitely not going to change the fundamentals of its approach to organising and making the world's information accessible and useful. Google's investment in its search technology is considerable and there is little chance of its shifting away from the fundamental approach that relies on the Reputation it calculates from the Wisdom of Crowds, and on the Visibility and Relevance of the information it finds. As a result, we are confident that the guidelines in this book will remain valid and helpful for the foreseeable future, and while some of the details may have cause to embarrass us when we read them in years to come, we do not doubt that the fundamentals will hold true.

---

[1] http://www.google.co.uk/support/webmasters/bin/answer.py?hl=en&answer=35769

[2] http://www.google.com/support/webmasters/bin/answer.py?hl=en&answer=35291

APPENDIX 1: SHOULD YOU GET HELP IN?

Building a better website so that it acquires more of Google's love is frequently a significant undertaking for a business, whether it is being built from scratch or as an improvement to an existing one. Not only is it significant, but it also requires a set of skills that rarely exist in one place. The skills required to build the sort of site we have evangelised about throughout this book are a combination of technical, editorial, marketing and relationship-building all immersed in the experience of working with and on the web. A hard job that requires a special combination of skills seems to cry out for external help – we've yet to encounter a website that couldn't do with a bit of it – but, you will be pleased to hear, it is not simply a choice between external help or Google rejection!

If this book has not left you with a ream of actions that you should already be getting on with, without any further external support, then we have failed to empower you with sufficient knowledge and confidence to make you roll up your sleeves and get to work. There are many basic activities that do not require much skill and effort to make Google love your site just that little bit more. Many of the details in the previous chapters will have given the more professional web managers among you bigger tasks, and more involved projects, but these actions do not require the services of an external provider, only the talents that exist within your current team.

Despite your new empowerment, you may still prefer to have an expert come in and organise things. There is no doubt that an appropriately skilled practitioner will make your life a whole lot easier on the Google love front, but, as with all such decisions, does it make sense to employ one, and if so, in what form?

So, while you can get on with some things straight away, deciding whether you can justify help for the other, more challenging, tasks requires an answer to the following question:

- How much value can you get from a significant increase in visits to your website – say a 100% increase – over the next 12 months?

Answering this question requires a basic knowledge of how much an average web visit is worth to your operation, which in simple terms will be the average profit per transaction divided by the average number of visits it takes to your website before a purchase is made (if you don't have a transactional website, you will need some other equivalent to a 'purchase' – perhaps a lead submitted via a web form, or a telephone call traced back to a visit to the site)[1]. If you are planning a new site and have no existing visits to calculate from, double your planned-for levels of profit from the site and use that figure[2].

Double the profit. 100% more visits. Are we serious? Well, yes, we are. While not every website we've worked on has enjoyed a doubling of visits as a result of increasing Google's love, there are many that have experienced much more. The larger businesses with very well-established brands and sites find it hardest to achieve such levels of growth, but even there, if the site has not had any other work done to improve the levels of natural search-referred visits from Google, performance increases of well over 100% are possible. The 100% increase figure is mainly intended to help you estimate the resources you

---

[1] Revisit chapter 6 Using Google to Grow: Better Lovin'.

[2] If you haven't got any of these figures or can't work them out, then you are really flying free, and we're not sure we want to be held even slightly accountable for what you do next.

may be able to make available to recruit external helpers, and to help you decide if it's at all feasible. And on the assumption that you have completed this estimation process and found the figure to be in excess of £10,000[1], over 12 months, then keep reading.

If your figure is less than £10,000, your website is clearly not the core revenue generator of your business, or it is a bit of a hobby or a smaller second income. Our advice would be to decide whether it can be a more significant earner, and what sort of resources will it need to become one, before you contemplate paying someone to help you with SEO. Once that decision is made, you will know whether you can invest further in your site or whether you are going to have to continue with the do-it-yourself approach. It is better to have your feet on the ground than to have a fantasy about the sort of business you are and spend money you can't afford. If you can't afford cash, but are prepared to invest more of your time in your site, then this book will continue to help you directly, so keep reading and rereading it. If it hasn't got the specific answer to your question, then visit Appendix 2: Useful Stuff, where we have compiled a list of places and resources where you can find communities and literature that will provide further help.

WHAT DOES SEO HELP LOOK LIKE?

Assuming you have passed the £10,000 test in the previous section, what sorts of search engine optimisation (SEO) services might you be able to secure in the marketplace to help you with your Google love problem? Well, you are going to find two main types of assistance from hungry suppliers ready to bite your hands off, and they are:

---

[1] The larger businesses among you can stop scoffing now. Of course you are going to generate more than £10,000 extra revenue if you double your visits and you've probably already spoken to an external supplier or two about SEO help. Regardless, there will still be plenty of you who haven't got a clue what your average value per visit is.

1. Consultancies who will work with you to identify the strategic and tactical opportunities in your market and how best to use SEO methods to develop your website – and your operations, including knowledge transfer and training – to take advantage of them.
2. Agencies who will unburden you of the day-to-day worry of Google's love and act as either an outsource partner or a virtual team member to deliver practical daily pursuit of free visitors from Google.

The business models of these types of SEO supplier are typically quite different: the consultancies will charge a high hourly rate for their input, which tends to be front-loaded, but which tails off as your confidence and knowledge reach a critical point; the agencies will look to commit you to a monthly retained fee for a minimum period (usually 12 months) while they provide services and act on your behalf.

One of these models may suit you more than the other, depending on your appetite for learning and your own business model. We have an opinion about which we believe is best for business – considering the importance of Google – which is reflected in the business model we present as a supplier, but we don't intend to prejudice you against the other, and are trying to be as neutral about it as we can because both these models have a role in the marketplace. So the decision you must make now, before approaching either type is:

- Do I want my team to learn and acquire the skills to grow Google's love for my site for themselves?
- Am I happy to rely on an outsider to develop Google's love for my site by proxy?

CHOOSING AN SEO SUPPLIER

The underpinning of most successful business relationships is trust. SEO relationships are no different. So, more than anything else you see or hear from the prospective suppliers you meet, you must feel that they really do appear to know what they are talking about and that they are going to have your best interests at heart. These judgements are difficult to make without any sort of history in a relationship, so it is essential that your engagement of a supplier has an option for the relationship to be reviewed and terminated early on. There is no substitute for being an informed customer, so you are doing the right thing reading this book first, but you should also read Google's own advice again[1].

Most SEO suppliers will employ sales people whose job it is to sell you services. These sales people are usually remunerated in line with their success in selling, which sadly means they are motivated primarily by their self-interest and only secondarily by your interests. This is not a problem unique to the search engine services marketplace, obviously, but when the gap between the supplier's knowledge and the customer's knowledge is as big as it typically is where Google's love is concerned, it has the potential to really mess things up. The best way to avoid such problems is to not only meet sales people. Insist instead that your initial contact and meetings are with representatives of the services you will actually be engaging, such as project consultants or strategy advisers or developers or even the CEO. Don't waste your own time meeting anyone who refuses this request, however politely.

Specialist or Bolt-on

The supply of SEO services typically comes from specialist SEO firms (or Search Engine Marketing firms) who focus on search engine services for natural and paid search, and from agencies that have bolted on an SEO service to their other digital marketing or web design proposition. On the balance of probability you are going to get a better service from the specialist

---

[1] http://www.google.com/support/webmasters/bin/answer.py?hl=en&answer=35291

firms, because they are dedicated to this area and are able to recruit specifically for talent suited to their services. Agencies find themselves attempting to recruit SEO specialists into existing pay scales and management structures where the focus of the business is elsewhere, and when their knowledge of SEO is usually inadequate to make a good appointment in the first place. Because demand for the best SEO talent is outstripping supply, agencies typically miss out and end up recruiting individuals who may have a good basic knowledge but will find themselves out of their depth when dealing with the finer intricacies of Google's love. These are generalisations, naturally, which come from many years of working in both agency environments and in our own practices, and which doubtless cannot be true for all suppliers.

Obfuscation and Snake Oil; Chinese Medicine and Love Potions

No-one can guarantee that you will be number one in Google. If a supplier offers such a guarantee, it's best to walk away. Really, don't even bother to ask about the conditions, because Google's natural results are un-guaranteeable. Period. And this will be a waste of your precious time.

As we said in the Introduction, the frontier town of SEO is full of snake oil[1] salesmen, so you need to be on your guard. There are no elixirs or love potions available that will magically attract Google to your site, and the pursuit of such short cuts is a slippery slope towards Google's rejection[2]. As with most things in life, if it appears too good to be true, then it probably is. SEO suppliers who attempt to sell you stuff without being prepared

---

[1] With apologies to those who really do sell snake oil for therapeutic purposes, on which we hesitate to have an opinion.

[2] http://www.google.com/support/webmasters/bin/answer.py?hl=en&answer=35843

to tell you exactly what it is in it – in other words, what they are planning to do to your site – are charlatans. Presented as trade secrets, such obfuscation makes a mockery of the good, sensible and transparent work that many suppliers do in this marketplace. So, again, if they will not offer such transparency, don't talk to them.

Fees and the Cost of Getting Help In

The fees SEO suppliers charge can be grouped loosely along the following lines:

1. Time-based, hourly rates, estimated in advance, billed in arrears.
2. Retained monthly fees designed to cover most activities, minimum contracts usually 12 months.
3. Success-based payments, calculated on agreed measures of increased SEO performance.

Occasionally arrangements include a combination of either 1 and 3 or 2 and 3. The models have their advantages and disadvantages, and only you'll know which works best for your organisation:

Model	Advantage	Disadvantage
Time	Pay only for the work that is pre-agreed and completed.	Cash-flow intensive, with larger fees due earlier.
Retainer	Predictable cash-flow.	Long commitment that often costs more. Low time accountability.
Success	Pay only when traffic increases.	Difficulties in measuring SEO cause and effect.

The only further comment we'll make at this point is that SEO measurement, and its association with the cause and effect the supplier is claiming, is notoriously difficult. While success fees are a very attractive model for both parties, you, as the buyer with little experience of SEO measurement, are subject to potential manipulation by a supplier tempted by the rewards that will come from a success model.

SELF-SUFFICIENCY: TRAINING AND RECRUITING

If you've read this entire book, you will not have been able to escape our belief that SEO for Google is a core demand for organisations to address. SEO is by its nature multidisciplinary. For it to work effectively, it must combine the pursuit of technical excellence with a determination to meet the needs of a market and an energetic desire to build peerless word-of-mouth recommendations. In fact SEO is online business in a microcosm and its effective delivery needs a shared vision and collaboration for it to succeed. Shared vision across technical, editorial and marketing disciplines is rare, and almost never spontaneous, but it must exist in some form before SEO can be expected to deliver.

We also believe that you should be striving towards self-sufficiency for the majority of your needs to acquire Google's love. This isn't an in-house/outsource argument; this is a push towards search becoming a key organisational discipline that needs to be embraced by the operations that are able to affect it. The multidisciplinary nature of SEO forces oversight of it up the organisation chart and into the executive. Recruiting a relatively junior SEO specialist into the marketing or technical team would be like giving up your seat on the bus for Google and expecting it to fall passionately in love with you as a result. When Google is being courted by a million Romeos every day who employ every romantic and seductive technique imaginable, you would find yourself nowhere near Google's field of vision, let alone its heart.

The pursuit of Google's love is an organisation-wide effort that needs a number of different strands of training and probably recruitment. Depending on your organisation's business model, or its modus operandi, some of the skills required may be more important than others. For example, website design and construction is often outsourced, which will mean that much of the technical skill will not be required in-house; however, an ability to understand the nature of technical work must be anchored within your organisation.

Typical training and recruitment efforts, in our experience, fall into the following categories:

1. Overview explanations about the way Google works and what Google is likely to think about your site.
2. Technical workshops on Visibility, structure and Reputation flow.
3. Training in user demand research and content creation.
4. Creative workshops for destination and link bait content production.
5. Real reputation development training, including social media engagement.
6. Training to institutionalise action-based web traffic analysis.

Training of this nature is best coordinated by team members who aren't beginners in SEO but are part-way there already. If you don't have such people, now is the time to think about recruiting them. And, good luck with that. As with the supplier in the previous section, it is not going to be easy for you to find, evaluate and afford the sort of people you probably need. Actually, what are we saying? You *will* be able to afford them. The money will not be the problem. The problem will most likely be a political one where the appointment needs more influence, power and money than the existing executive is prepared to give it. We're sorry if this sounds cynical, but the same thing happened in the late 1990s when businesses really needed to bring experienced e-commerce people into their teams to exploit the rapidly growing online retail channels, but were not prepared to squeeze them into the existing management structures, so they typically got what they deserved, which was less experienced, less effective, less costly second fiddles. The impact on their e-commerce effectiveness was disastrous, adding years to their approximation of e-commerce best practice.

The time is right to promote the experienced and expensive search specialists into leading roles within organisations. Their ability to explain the relationship between what is done operationally and Google's love, and their coordination of the varied skills required, provide the impetus organisations need to chase after that huge chunk of the marketplace currently mediated by Google. And if you think we are guilty of self-serving rhetoric, you are right, but probably not for the reason you think. Our experience of working with organisations is profoundly better when the coordinating force within the business is Google-literate and has some prior experience of SEO, which helps us and increases our job satisfaction. Those organisations that take the plunge to pursue Google's love by using SEO in new roles find opportunities opening up for them much quicker than if they resist such change.

APPENDIX 2: USEFUL STUFF

OFFICIAL GOOGLE RESOURCES

Google Webmaster Central: http://www.google.co.uk/webmasters/

Google Webmaster Tools: http://www.google.com/webmasters/tools/

Google Webmaster YouTube Channel:
   http://www.youtube.co.uk/GoogleWebmasterHelp

Google Webmaster Blog: http://googlewebmastercentral.blogspot.com/

Google Webmaster Help Forum:
   http://www.google.com/support/forum/p/Webmasters

(Take care here. Do not assume because you read advice on Google's own forum that it is official or correct.)

Google Webmaster SEO advice:
   http://www.google.com/support/webmasters/bin/answer.py?hl=en&answer=35291

UNOFFICIAL GOOGLE RESOURCES

Matt Cutts, Head of Google's Webspam Team: http://www.mattcutts.com/blog/

Google Blogoscoped: http://blogoscoped.com/

SEO RESOURCES

WebmasterWorld: http://www.webmasterworld.com/

Search Engine Land: http://searchengineland.com/

Search Engine Watch: http://searchenginewatch.com/

SEOmoz: http://www.seomoz.org/

Econsultancy SEO Best Practice Guide: http://econsultancy.com/reports/search-engine-optimization-seo-best-practice-guide (Steve is an expert reviewer)

SUPPLIER SOURCES

Econsultancy Search Marketing SEO Supplier Directory:
http://econsultancy.com/directories/suppliers/topics/seo

GENERAL TECHNICAL RESOURCES

World Wide Web Consortium (W3C), Accessibility Guidelines:
http://www.w3.org/TR/WCAG20/
W3C HTML Validator: http://validator.w3.org/
Web Standards Project: http://www.webstandards.org/
Wikipedia Article on Regular Expressions:
http://en.wikipedia.org/wiki/Regular_expression
CSV Easy: http://www.tizma.com/csveasy/
Wikipedia Article on Redirections: http://en.wikipedia.org/wiki/URL_redirection

SEARCH DATA RESOURCES

Google Keyword Tool (data provenance: its own hundreds of millions of daily searches): https://adwords.google.co.uk/select/KeywordToolExternal
Experian Hitwise (data provenance: licensed from ISPs, UK focused): http://www.hitwise.com/uk/
Word Tracker (date provenance: licensed from Dogpile search engine, US focused): http://www.wordtracker.com/
Keyword Discovery (data provenance: user panel through toolbar, US focused): http://www.keyworddiscovery.com
Wordze (data provenance: licensed from ISPs and toolbar panel, US focused): http://www.wordze.com/

BOOKS

Amy Langville and Carl Meyer, *Google's PageRank and Beyond*, Princeton University Press, 2006.
John Battelle, *The Search*, Nicholas Brearley Publishing, 2005.
Chris Anderson, *The Long Tail*, Random House, 2006.

James Surowiecki, *The Wisdom of Crowds: Why the Many Are Smarter Than the Few and How Collective Wisdom Shapes Business, Economies, Societies and Nations*, Little, Brown, 2004.

Malcolm Gladwell, *The Tipping Point: How Little Things Can Make A Big Difference*, Little, Brown, 2000.

David A. Vise, *The Google Story*, Delta, 2008.

Enge, Spencer, Fishkin, Stricchiola, *The Art of SEO*, O'Reilly, 2010.

MISCELLANEOUS RESOURCES

Wordnet: http://wordnetweb.princeton.edu/perl/webwn

APPENDIX 3: GLOSSARY

AdWords Google's pay-per-click adverts which are presented above and to the right of the main results of a Google search.

Analytics The measuring of all sorts of things about how a website is used – where visitors came from, what they read, how long they spent, where they went afterwards, and much more besides!

apps Apps are 'software applications' – things you can install on your computer (or phone). Web apps are like apps but you don't need to install them, you just run them through your web browser (this experience of running apps over the web is called 'cloud computing' by the more excitable technophiles out there). *See* GOOGLE APPS for a specific example.

blockquote Longer quotations – paragraphs of copy taken from other websites, or books or papers – can be marked as such in HTML by surrounding them with blockquote tags: <blockquote>they look like this.</blockquote>.

blog Short for 'web log' – originally a website presenting a series of dated journal entries. Tends to consist of commentary, day to day experiences, information on hobbies, interests or obsessions, travel diaries, etc. It is also used as a verb, 'to blog' being to post some text, an image or a video to a blog.

bot Short for 'software robot' – a piece of software designed to carry out a simple and repetitive task, such as wandering around the WORLD WIDE WEB recording page content and links.

ccTLD   Country-code Top Level Domain – reserved for sovereign states, in theory. The 'uk' bit of '.co.uk'.

crawl   When applied to a BOT, crawling is the act of wandering around the WORLD WIDE WEB, recording page content and links.

CSS   Cascading Style Sheets – a language used to describe the layout, colours, background images and formatting of web pages.

CSV   Comma-separated values file – a simple database format that uses commas to separate fields and carriage-returns (new lines) to separate rows.

Dotcom   A company whose business is based around and through the WORLD WIDE WEB ('.com' denotes a commercial website domain as opposed to '.org' for a non-commercial organisation, for example).

filename   The name given to a computer file – usually consists of a name, a dot, and an extension such as 'bob.xls'. The extension tells you what kind of file it is – an MS Word document gets a .doc file extension, for example, giving filenames such as 'my-document.doc'. Common filename extensions on the web include .htm, .html, .asp, .aspx, .css, .js, .pl .

Flash   Known variously as Shockwave Flash, Macromedia Flash and Adobe Flash through its history, Flash is a frame-based editing package for adding animation and interactivity to web pages. It includes a scripting language related to JAVASCRIPT called ActionScript. It was never really designed to be accessible or indexable, but every new version is a little better than the last.

Google Apps   Google Apps are a set of web-based software applications comprising a word processor, spreadsheets, presentation software, a calendar, and a few more bits and pieces. Google are not the only folks doing this sort of thing – Zoho Docs are also offering something similar (if not better), and Microsoft Office-in-the-cloud will be around shortly, if it isn't already by the time you are reading this.

Google Docs   Google's web-based word-processing application.

Google Webmaster Central   A Google site aimed at the folks who run websites, it includes blogs, forums and help groups, and a whole bunch of tools to help understand how Google sees the webmaster's own websites. *See* GOOGLE WEBMASTER TOOLS for more information.

Google Webmaster Tools   A free service for webmasters from Google. Shows problems detected by GOOGLEBOT while crawling your site, gives information on sites linking in to your site and on keywords used to search for your site, and much more besides.

Googlebot   One of many. Googlebots are pieces of software that request web pages from servers, read them, index them and look for links to follow.

http   Hypertext transfer protocol – the language that lets browsers talk to webservers.

hyperlink   A link from one HYPERTEXT file to another. Almost always applied to web pages, which are a type of hypertext file.

hypertext   Computer-readable text organised by links from one piece of text to another. Web pages are examples of pieces of hypertext.

ISP   Internet Service Provider – the folks at the other end of your modem, who let you on to the internet.

JavaScript   A scripting programming language most often used to add interactive features to web pages.

knoll   An entry in Google's 'knol' project – a unit of knowledge, contributed by an author with a proven expertise in the subject. The Knol project is Google's answer to Wikipedia. (However it does not seem to be making big waves on the web scene yet.)

mark-up   Annotations to text defining how it is to be laid out, structured or formatted. HTML is the mark-up used on web pages.

MP3   Short for MPEG-1 Audio Layer 3 – a digital audio file format used for music downloads, podcasts and more.

nofollow An instruction to search engines that a HYPERLINK should not be trusted and therefore not be allowed to influence the search engine's ranking of the link's target.

PageRank A way of measuring the relative importance of a web page. Invented by the founders of Google – Larry Page and Sergey Brin.

PDF Portable Document Format – a file format that allows documents to be passed around unaffected by operating systems, software or hardware. Great for print documents, but not as Google-friendly as normal HTML web pages.

personas Made-up characters created to represent typical users of a website or computer programme. Helps keep designers focused on the needs of the user.

pingback One of several methods of a web page (usually BLOG) author requesting notification when someone links to their web page. Can be used generically to apply to all such methods. Other methods include Linkback, Trackback and Refback, but they all do essentially the same thing.

Python A computer programming language. Very readable. Often used for writing web APPS – YouTube, for example.

Quicktime A proprietary multimedia framework from Apple. One of several methods of adding interactive video/audio to web pages.

Rails (or Ruby on Rails) A web application framework for the Ruby programming language used for putting web applications together. Basecamp and Twitter are examples of web applications that rely heavily on Ruby on Rails.

SEO Search Engine Optimisation – the process of increasing the volume and quality of traffic to a website from search engines. Also sometimes used as a noun for those who practice SEO, as in a Search Engine Optimiser.

singlecast Like broadcast, but to only one person.

Sitelinks Google's name for the links shown below some sites in its search results, representing the pages that Google thinks searchers will most want to visit within the site.

sitemaps   A protocol that allows webmasters to inform search engines about the pages on the webmaster's site, including, amongst other things, the relative importance that the webmaster believes the pages should have.

spam   Unsolicited or undesired electronic messages, and similar abuses in other media.

stylesheet   A set of instructions about the presentation and layout of a web page.

trackback   *See* PINGBACK.

URI, URL, URN   Any resource on the internet has a uniform address indentifier (URI) which can be a name (uniform resource name, or URN) or how to find it (uniform resource locator, or URL), or both. Perhaps the best known example of a URI is the web page address (such as www.searchjohnston. co.uk/about-us/index.php). In non-technical literature, where websites are mentioned, URL and URI are often used interchangeably – the need to distinguish between the two rarely arises.

webspam   Attempts to manipulate the Relevancy and Reputation calculations of a search engine, in a way that works against the intentions of the search engine.

world wide web   The set of all information accessible using computers and networking, each unit of information identified by a URI.

XHTML   Extensible HyperText Markup Language – a more formally structured, machine-friendly version of HTML.

INDEX